We had one of those too!

We had one of those too!

STEPHEN BARNETT

pb potton & burton

First published in 2018 by Potton & Burton

Potton & Burton
98 Vickerman Street, PO Box 5128, Nelson, New Zealand
pottonandburton.co.nz

ISBN 978 0 947503 91 8

Printed in China by Midas Printing International Ltd

Contents

Introduction

We Had One of Those Too! celebrates, as did an earlier volume, the marvellous cars seen along New Zealand's roads during the 1950s and 1960s. This new selection once again comprises models most Kiwis are likely to have been familiar with – cars that they or their parents or grandparents drove. Along with these are a few that were less common but added to a unique automotive range, and which also, for many, represented aspirational yearnings ... I'm thinking myself here of the Daimler SP250 and VW's Karmann Ghia. The SP250, or Dart, is one of a number of British sports cars to appear in the book; cars of a kind – nimble and exciting – not made anywhere else. Always interesting that a country known for its rain should have produced some of the most memorable open-top sports cars.

Cars – particularly new ones – were still special and something of a luxury in New Zealand in the 1950s, and we hadn't yet come to take for granted the personal mobility and freedom they offered. There was a greater fascination with cars then, and motoring itself was arguably more fun than now, what with modern-day traffic volumes, restrictions on parking and the like. We got our driving licence at 15, honed our drifting skills on gravel roads out of town, and did our own maintenance and minor repairs (aided by *Motoring with Robbie* each weekend on the radio). Rust was a particular problem in the days before the invention of really effective protection, and a lot of home car maintenance centred around cutting out rust holes and filling them with bog – some cars you saw seemed to be more fibreglass than steel.

And there were ways around other roadblocks to our enjoyment of driving. You may have drawn the line at buying a WOF sticker at the public bar of certain pubs, but surely if the authorities insisted on carless days, then buying a cheap old banger and giving it a sticker for a different day of the week to your main car was only reasonable?

What made the period unique when it came to cars was the remarkable diversity of styling and engineering. Taking advantage of the era's increasing prosperity, manufacturers provided the consumer with a steady stream of new cars offering the latest in comfort, handling, styling and increased power. The result was such

ABOVE A gallery of 1940s and 1950s models along Shortland Street, Auckland, 1953. The city's first parking meters are being installed. Half an hour's parking cost thruppence in those days.

OPPOSITE Members of a wedding party and their A40 Somerset; somewhere in Auckland, late 1950s–early 1960s.

67.091

LEFT Matamata street races sometime in the 1960s with a bevy of British sports cars dicing for the lead. A Triumph TR2 (or perhaps a TR3) is bringing up the rear behind a Triumph Spitfire, then ahead of that an Austin–Healey and at the front of the pack, a Daimler SP250.

OPPOSITE Cains Motors, Silverstream, Upper Hutt, mid-1960s. Opening day of the new service station with Atlantic oil company reps acting as service attendants for the day. The car at right is a Wolseley 4/44.

divergent models as the Jaguar E-type, Ford Corsair and Nash Metropolitan. (Often, however, when it came to styling, some manufacturers went too far, missing the truth that for consumers the first cut can often be the deepest, and insisting on evolving breakout first designs into bloated territory. You could argue that the response depended on your age, and at what point you 'entered' that design phase. If you were in your mid-teens, say, in the early 1970s, then a 1973 Mustang might look superior to a 1965 model ... although you would be wrong, of course.)

As in the earlier volume, the main feature of this book is the reproductions of pages from evocative sales brochures of the 1950s and 1960s, which prospective purchasers of the time would pore over. Cars were comparatively expensive then and buying a new one could be properly accomplished only after close study of such brochures and the information they contained relating to specifications and the manufacturer's claims – illustrated with seductive artwork – of the changes the new vehicle promised to bring to your life. The copywriting and design of these pamphlets often have a romance and whimsy that today's website approach sorely lacks. In addition they comprise an invaluable survey of the social history and technical and design trends of the decades.

Quoted material that appears throughout this book's text is largely drawn from these brochures.

Stephen Barnett

BRADFORD

10 CWT VAN ★ LORRY

SIX-SEATER UTILITY

JOWETT

JOWETT CARS LTD - BRADFORD & LONDON - ENGLAND

1946
Jowett Bradford

ALTHOUGH OF LATE 1940S TO EARLY 1950S MANUFACTURE, Bradford vans and trucks were still much in evidence throughout the 1960s, testament to their usefulness, economy and, not least, durability. They were surprisingly strong for what they were and seemed to go on for ever. Everything about the Bradford spoke of economy, even thrift (they were made in Yorkshire, after all), and their basic design and simple mechanicals (easily repaired) appealed in a post-war economy that was focused on avoiding unnecessary expenditure.

The Jowett motor company was based in Bradford, Yorkshire, and had made its start in light engineering and as a manufacturer of engines. These were almost all horizontally opposed twin-cylinders or fours, which were used as stationary engines.

The company had produced lightweight cars using their engines in the early years of the business, but it was with the production of the Bradford vans and lorries following World War II, along with the later Jowett Javelin and Jupiter cars (page 20), that the name became well known. The vans, first produced in 1946, came in a number of configurations. Initially, a simple 10 cwt van with only a driver's seat was produced (a front passenger seat was an option), which was subsequently joined by the Utility, an estate car that had more side windows and rear seats. Later, there was also a Utility '4-light van', which retained the windows but had no rear seats (in order to avoid the UK's purchase tax payable on private passenger vehicles), along with a 10 cwt lorry. In addition, the company sold chassis and cab-chassis versions to outside coachbuilders, who put their own bodies on them.

The Bradford van engine, a 1005 cc side-valve flat twin, was initially rated at 19 bhp; this was later improved to 25 bhp. These weren't fast vehicles by any means – a Utility De Luxe tested in 1952 managed a top speed of just 53 mph – and stories abound of their limitations, of the care that had to be taken when loading heavy goods into them as too much weight at the rear could lift the front wheels off the road, and of drivers having to reverse them up the steeper hills. The De Luxe was top of the range, with chromed headlights and grille surround, and two windscreen wipers.

ABOVE Members of the Mehrtens family and their Bradford, 1950s. Like a lot of Bradford vans, this one had windows inserted into the sides after purchase to make it more usable.

'Bradford thrives on hard labour.'

ABOVE Chaney's Four Square's Bradford delivery van, in front of the St Albans, Christchurch store, 1962. These little, flat-twin powered vans were incredibly strong and durable while their large flat sides provided lots of space for signwriting. A number of Four Square stores in Christchurch ran Bradfords as their delivery vans at this time.

In New Zealand, imported Bradfords were assembled by the Turner brothers at a building in Greys Avenue in Auckland. The vehicles came in as a bare chassis, with only the front mudguards, bonnet and scuttle to the top of the windscreen. The rest of the body was then built by the importers or, as in the UK, by other coachbuilders, which is why the vans appeared in so many body designs and fabrication types.

The BRADFORD thrives on hard labour

THE BRADFORD VAN

Designed for a 10 cwt. payload with a capacity of 93 cubic feet, yet to give all the economy of an 8 h.p. engine. With low unladen weight, yet extremely strong with bonded metal body. For light bulky loads 8 cwt. springs may be specified when ordering. Extras: Painting in green, blue or grey; passenger's seat.

WHEN the JOWETT factory at Idle, Bradford, Yorkshire, had finished its War work, immediate steps were taken to put into production again a range of light commercial vehicles. These are now known as the BRADFORD range which consists of the 10 cwt. Van, the drop-side Lorry, the six-seater Utility and six-light Van, together with a de luxe range consisting of the Utility and Van. (Please see separate leaflet for de luxe models.)

The BRADFORD chassis follows the general lines of the well-known pre-war models (many of which have done 250,000 miles and more), but it has been considerably strengthened and the water-cooled horizontally opposed twin-cylinder engine has been redesigned to give a greater power output. Now rated at 8 h.p., this 1,005 c.c. unit develops 19 b.h.p. at 3,500 r.p.m., and is notable for its solid construction and simplicity, its hard working qualities and high power output at low engine speeds. Owing to the big bearing surfaces and the fewer moving parts which this flat twin design permits, longer life, greater economy and consistent reliability are ensured.

The JOWETT factory has been producing horizontally opposed water-cooled twins since 1906 and, as the testing ground is the wild country of the Yorkshire moors, a very hardy vehicle has been developed, suitable for use in any part of the world. The Bradford has already won a permanent overseas market and is backed by a world-wide spares service.

THE BRADFORD LORRY

The ideal Builders' or Merchants' open truck with 27 square feet of loading space, drop sides and rear panel. Immensely strong. Extras: Painting in green, blue or grey; passenger's seat.

THE BRADFORD 10 CWT. VAN

THE BRADFORD CHASSIS

For special body purposes the BRADFORD chassis can be supplied either as a 'drive-away' chassis (fitted with a temporary box seat) or as a 'cab' chassis which has the cab fitting complete and is ready for the body-builder behind the cab.

BRADFORDS FOR EXPORT

All BRADFORDS are available with left-hand steering and metric instruments for export. Overseas BRADFORDS are fitted with Export air cleaners.

THE BRADFORD 10 CWT. LORRY

THE BRADFORD SIX-LIGHT VAN - in green, blue or grey, with passenger's seat, or in primer

THE BRADFORD SIX-SEATER UTILITY for the export market - This interior view shows the excellent accommodation.

General Information

ENGINE AND CHASSIS

Bore	3⅛ in. (79.4 mm.)
Stroke	4 in. (101.6 mm.)
Swept volume	1,005 c.c
Licensing weight	14 cwt. 723 Kg.
Power output	19 b.h.p. at 3,500 r.p.m.
Wheelbase	7 ft. 6 in. 228.5 cm.
Track	4 ft. 0½ in. 123.2 cm.
Gear-box	3-speed and Reverse
Ratios—Top	4.89 : 1
2nd	9.3 : 1
1st	18.1 : 1
Rev.	24.7 : 1
Turning circle	34 ft. 10.35 m.
Ignition	Coil, 6 volt battery
Petrol tank capacity	5½ gallons 25 litres
Tyres	5.00 × 16 in.
Wheels	2.75 × 16 in.
Ground clearance	7½ in. 19 cm.

VAN AND UTILITY

Width inside	4 ft. 6 in.	137 cm.
Width between arches	3 ft. 3¼ in.	99.7 cm.
Length inside behind driver's seat	4 ft. 9½ in.	146 cm.
Length of floor	5 ft. 3½ in.	161 3 cm.
Max. inside length	9 ft. 0 in.	274 cm.
Max. height inside	3 ft. 9½ in.	115.6 cm.
Loading height	22½ in.	57.1 cm.
Width door opening	3 ft. 11 in.	119.4 cm.
Height door opening	3 ft. 4 in.	101.6 cm.
Capacity behind seat	78 cu. ft.	2.152 cu. m.
Capacity driver's cab	15 cu. ft.	.368 cu. m.
Floor space	20 sq. ft.	1.87 sq. m.
Overall length	12 ft. 0 in.	368.7 cm.
Overall width	5 ft. 0 in.	152.4 cm.
Overall height (loaded)	5 ft. 9 in.	175.2 cm.

LORRY BODY

Platform	5 ft. 6 in. × 4 ft. 11 in.	168 cm. × 150 cm.
Platform area	27 sq ft.	2.52 sq. m.

THE BRADFORD SIX-SEATER UTILITY OR 6-LIGHT VAN

To meet the needs of those requiring extra passenger accommodation—as a station wagon, shooting brake or personnel car—the Six-Seater Utility has been introduced. The body of the Utility—which has four windows in each side—is of the same spacious dimensions as the Van (93 cubic feet) and has the four extra passenger seats staggered at each side of the wide centre aisle for maximum leg room. They are quickly detachable for carrying bulky loads. This vehicle is available as a van without rear seats. The 8 cwt. springs are fitted. Price includes painting in grey, blue or green.

ECONOMY - LONG LIFE - BIG LOADS - RELIABILITY - SIMPLICITY - STRENGTH

J.C/O 9450

ABOVE Before the advent of other commercial vans such as the Morris Minor and the Morris J, Bradfords were the mainstay of light commercial delivery, despite the fact that they were neither hugely powerful nor fast.

1947
Austin A40 Devon

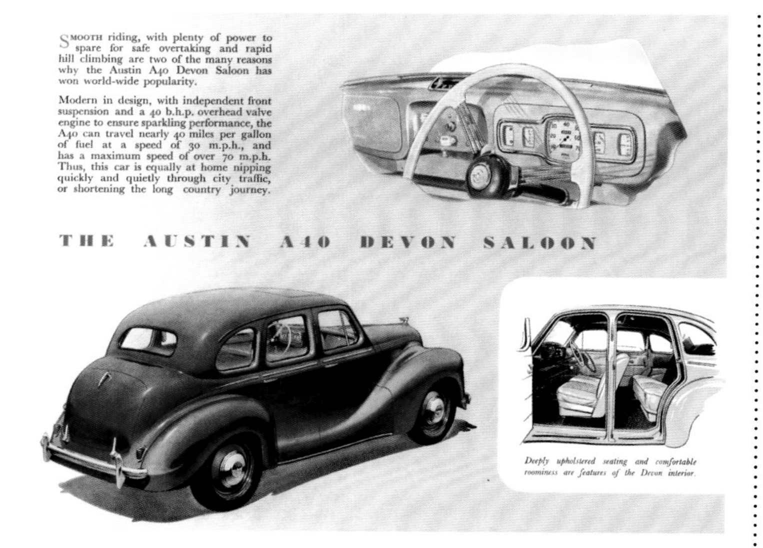

ABOVE The A40 Devon was a 4-door model and proved more popular than its 2-door Dorset sister.

THE A40 WAS A LINE OF TOUGH CARS that always seemed to be present in the background of my childhood and teenage years. By the 1970s, a lot of the old A40s were still going strong, although of increasingly little value, the kind of car teenagers could pick up cheaply and that never owed you much.

Convertible models were rare. I remember a group of us deciding to convert a friend's A40 bomb to a convertible one sunny weekend, an exercise that ended up involving hacksaws, hammers and much rending of metal, along with the realisation that windows needed a roof at the tops of A and B pillars in order to be wound up and down. That aside, the conversion was wholly successful – if you accepted the lack of any real convertible top and instead were happy to tie down blue plastic sheeting with rope when it rained.

The Austin Motor Company marketed a number of different cars under the A40 label from 1947. At that time, the company's naming system was based on the approximate engine output, and to avoid confusion, models were also given names – these were often derived from English counties. The 4-door A40 Devon and its short-lived 2-door A40 Dorset sister were Austin's first new models following the end of World War II, and the Devon was very successful. This was due in part to the pent-up demand for cars that couldn't be satisfied through the war years, and in part because the Devon offered a lot of car for the money. Solidly engineered and built, it was a car that kept going under fairly harsh treatment, and if the styling wasn't exactly groundbreaking (in Austin's desire to get back into production quickly after the end of hostilities, the company carried over the conservative styling of its cars of the previous decade), it was reassuring. More than 450,000 were built before the model was replaced in 1952 by the A40 Somerset.

In addition to the basic saloon, the Devon model range comprised a van, a pick-up truck and the versatile Countryman estate: 'Although styled the "Countryman" and ideally suited to work on the estate and farm, this A40 passenger or goods-carrying model is quite at home in the town where its lively performance and manoeuvrability simplify the negotiation of traffic-congested streets.'

AUSTIN — for sparkling performance
A 40 DEVON SALOON

ABOVE A40 Pick-up truck had an open bed.

OPPOSITE Despite their old-fashioned appearance, the Devon and Dorset A40s were reasonably well powered by their 1.2-litre B-block 4-cylinder engines, the original flathead-four now enlivened with overhead valves. The top speed was about 70 mph.

There was also an A40 Sports, which, while not exactly a sports car, did allow for something more exciting than the basic A40 mechanicals. The Sports boasted twin carbs on the basic 1.2-litre Devon engine, giving a boost to power and producing a solid 80 mph top speed. The stylish body was made of aluminium.

In New Zealand, A40 Devons were assembled from complete knock-down kits at the Austin plant in Petone.

The rear mounting of the engine and gear box assembly

A cutaway view of the box section frame member

The same robust chassis is employed on all A40 commercial models. The frame, built-up of welded pressed-steel box-section side members securely cross-braced at the centre, provides rigid support for the assembled components, and a firm foundation for all styles of bodywork.

Released only from inside the car, the bonnet can be lifted up to give easy access to the engine.

The lid of the capacious boot hinges down to provide a platform for additional luggage.

The all steel body of the A40 Devon is sound insulated and has safe rear opening doors with concealed hinges and running boards. Softly upholstered seating, with individual close-mounted front seats, affords ample room and comfort for four adults, while generous accommodation for luggage is provided in an enclosed rear boot.

The Devon has a high-lustre finish and is available in a variety of colours. Seating, carpets, instruments and controls are all *en suite*, to give an air of modern elegance and refinement.

AUSTIN A 40

VAN · PICK-UP · COUNTRYMAN

for

- ★ DEPENDABLE SERVICE
- ★ ECONOMICAL OPERATION
- ★ LIVELY PERFORMANCE
- ★ CONFIDENT CONTROL
- ★ SMOOTH RIDING
- ★ STURDY CONSTRUCTION
- ★ EASY LOADING
- ★ LARGE GOODS CAPACITY

DESIGNED to give dependable service and built to last longer, the Austin A40 light commercials are without equal for transporting loads up to half-a-ton. On long or short journeys, through town traffic or in the country, over well-made surfaces or "roughing it", these sturdy vehicles will deliver the goods safely, speedily and economically.

The range comprises a closed van or "Panel Delivery," a "Pick-Up" open truck and a "Countryman" passenger-carrying van—three models which will not only undertake with distinction a great variety of light transport jobs, but by their handsome appearance will enhance the prestige of any business.

1½ litre
JAVELIN
BY JOWETT OF BRADFORD

1947
Jowett Javelin

THE JOWETT MOTOR COMPANY WAS A HIGHLY INNOVATIVE CAR MANUFACTURER based in Bradford, Yorkshire. Founded by two brothers in 1901, it made its start in light engineering and constructing light cars powered by the company's own flat-twin engines. Lorries and vans followed – famously the doughty Bradford van (page 10).

The Jowett Javelin was released in 1947 to a very positive reception. At a time when most British manufacturers were basically offering pre-war models, Jowett was selling a wholly new car for the mid-range market. The Javelin was well thought out and notable for such innovative features as the flat 4-cylinder, horizontally opposed cast-aluminium engine, and for the handsome aerodynamic styling, which included the headlights faired into the wings. The 1486 cc overhead-camshaft motor produced an effortless top speed of 80 mph – the Javelin was a class winner in the 1949 Monte Carlo Rally.

Over the Javelin's production life a number of models were manufactured, each with Standard and De Luxe versions. All were characterised by the Javelin's excellent handling, sporting performance and spacious interior – the shorter space occupied by the engine allowed greater leg room for passengers than would have been available with the more usual inline engine configuration.

One variant was the very stylish Jupiter sports car of 1950, powered by the same engine as the parent car but now tuned for greater speed and acceleration: 'The Jupiter will accelerate to 60 mph in approximately 15 seconds, reach over 90 mph and cruise at 80 mph as a matter of course, handling the whole time with the precision and safety that make it the prized possession of a man who understands what high speed motoring should be.' A Jupiter had a class win at the 1950 Le Mans, and enjoyed a class one–two at the following year's Monte Carlo Rally.

ABOVE A Jowett Javelin alongside what looks like a very early Jowett car, across the road from Jowett Motors in Greys Avenue, Auckland, late 1940s. In the background, at left, can be seen a couple of Bradford vans.

JAVELIN SALOON DE LUXE MODELS

The dignified colours—metallic grey and black are available in the de luxe range of saloons in addition to the maroon and turquoise models illustrated—set off the fine finish

'The Javelin's smooth, elegant lines are aerodynamically correct for easy passage through the air. Flush fitting headlights, recessed door handles and curved windscreen also mean silent, economical speed.' The new 1951 Javelin Saloon and Javelin De Luxe models came with a wider choice of colours and 'lavish equipment' that included a spotlight and windscreen demister.

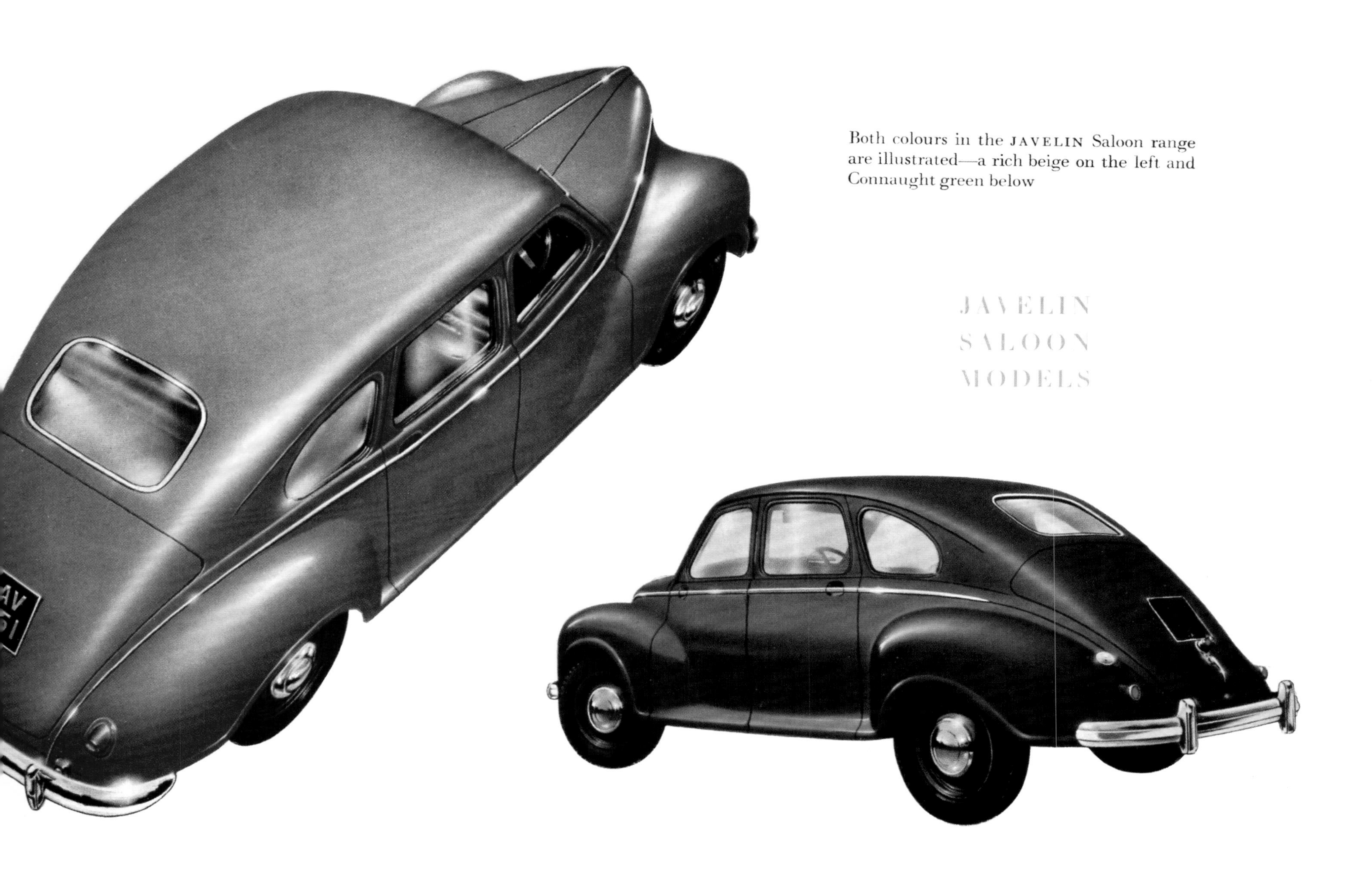

Both colours in the JAVELIN Saloon range are illustrated—a rich beige on the left and Connaught green below

JAVELIN SALOON MODELS

THE JAVELIN combines many characteristics which had previously belonged to widely varying types of car—the roominess of a family car; the comfort of a high-priced limousine; the road manners of a sports model; the acceleration of a big American car and a top speed of over 75 m.p.h. At the same time this compact car is notable for its economy, giving 29–33 m.p.g. under average conditions.

Because of these qualities the JAVELIN has won a fine reputation all over the world and has gained not only outstanding competition successes (winner 1½–litre class, Monte Carlo Rally 1949; winner in 1949 2–litre touring class Belgian 24 hour Grand Prix—1570 miles at 65·5 m.p.h.; outright winner Rallye des Neiges, Switzerland 1950), but a fine reputation for comfort, economy, reliability and hard work.

TWO MODELS—THE JAVELIN SALOON & SALOON DE LUXE

In the new 1951 models there is a wider choice of equipment, colour and detail specification. The JAVELIN saloon is available to the owner who wants the JAVELIN performance but who is willing to dispense with de luxe appointments on the coachwork side. The JAVELIN is also marketed in de luxe form, with a wide choice of colours and lavish equipment to satisfy the most exacting demands. In Great Britain there are over 200 qualified service agents and all our overseas distributors maintain nation-wide spare parts organisations and the majority employ Jowett trained mechanics.

JOWETT CARS LTD., Works: Idle, Bradford, Yorkshire (Tel. Idle 341). Showrooms: 48 Albemarle Street, London, W.1 (Tel. Regent 0721).

interior of the JAVELIN saloon

You will approve of the well-planned layout of this roomy car, which is remarkable for the amount of space given to both front and *rear* seat passengers. Plenty of leg room, a flat floor front and rear, and real inter-axle seating are main features. The base of the rear seat squab is actually 15 inches in front of the rear axle. Essential instruments are grouped in front of the driver, and both driver and passengers notice the remarkable all-round vision. The interior upholstery is in beige plastic and cloth—or all-plastic for export—good looking and extremely hardwearing.

The Javelin Saloon De Luxe had a spacious and highly finished interior.

1½ litre JO

the ca

The Jupiter chassis is of tubular construction, immensely strong.

The instrument layout is neat and legible. Forward visibility is excellent.

The clean imposing lines of the Jupiter arouse admiration everywhere it goes.

ETT JUPITER

at leaped to fame

'he Jowett Jupiter was especially built to give the nest all round high-speed motoring—startling cceleration, high cruising speed, economy and superb oad holding *plus* comfort in all weathers. Today e name Jupiter ranks high. In a very short time it as proved outstanding in the 1½ litre class. Consider these triumphs—

1950

e Mans 24 Hour Grand Prix d'Endurance 1½ litre Class
st: driven by T. H. Wisdom and T. C. Wise, breaking the ourse record at 75·8 m.p.h.

1951

Monte Carlo Rally 1½ litre Class
st: W. H. Robinson and R. Ellison.
nd: G. Wilkins and R. F. Baxter.

isbon Rally
st: in general classification and 1½ litre Class. J. Nogueira.

remgarten Sports Car Race 1½ litre Class
st: Herr Gurzeler.

heineck/Walzenhausen Hill Climb 1½ litre Class
st: Herr Gurzeler.

e Mans 24 Hour Grand Prix d'Endurance 1½ litre Class
st: M. Becquart and G. Wilkins at 71·9 m.p.h.

allye de L'Iseran
st: in general classification. M. Armengaud.

.A.C. Tourist Trophy Race. 1½ litre Class
st: H. L. Hadley at 68.71 m.p.h.
nd: T. C. Wise at 68.59 m.p.h.

Vatkins Glen, U.S.A. 1½ litre Race
st: George Weaver at 68.95 m.p.h.

In its First Race—Le Mans 1950—the only Jupiter entered won the 1½ litre class at the record speed of 75·8 m.p.h., driven by T. H. Wisdom and T. C. Wise.

Again in 1951 the Jupiter won the 1½ litre class at Le Mans and was the only car in the class to finish this gruelling 24 hour event. Driven by Gordon Williams and Marcel Becquart.

Before the 1951 Monte Carlo Rally, co-drivers Bill Robinson and Bob Ellison with their Jupiter—in its first international rally.

After Monte Carlo. Jupiters were 1st and 2nd in the 1½ litre class and with a Javelin saloon which finished 4th earned the manufacturers' team prize.

1947
Renault 4CV

ABOVE A Renault 4CV with its vented, sloped rear, seen in this photograph taken at the Ellerslie Races in Auckland, 1950s.

WHEN I FIRST SAW THE RENAULT 4CV, I wasn't sure if I was looking at a VW variant, so similar is its shape – in particular the rear of the car – to the German Beetle. It was a stylish piece of design, with a roofline that swept back over the engine and with louvred cooling vents at the rear. Details included air intakes set at the front edges of the rear guards, and an art deco surround to the radiator cap (4CV drivers had to stay vigilant when pulling up at petrol pumps to ensure that service-station attendants didn't mistake the radiator cap for the petrol cap). Such touches added to the appeal of the 4CV and gave it an air of foreignness.

The Renault 4CV was a rear-engine, rear-wheel-drive car – again, similar to the Beetle, although it had a water-cooled engine rather than the air cooling of the VW. It was conceived as a small, economical car for the period of austerity expected in France following the end of World War II. In this it was successful. The 4CV was inexpensive to buy, both economical to run and maintain, and it looked good: 'The aerodynamic shape of the 750 combines elegance of line with the best streamlining and drag coefficient of any 4-seater saloon in the world.' Thanks to its all-round independent suspension, it also handled well on a variety of road surfaces. More than a million Renault 4CVs were built over its 14-year lifespan.

At the time of its introduction, the 4CV attracted the nickname 'lump of butter' for its shape and the sand-yellow colour of its paintwork – the paint was said to be surplus stock from German Afrika Korps military vehicles.

The 760 cc engine of the first 4CVs generated 18 bhp; following years saw the power output increased to 21.5 hp, enabling a top speed of about 60 mph. The engine was notable also for its torque and flexibility, with top gear usable for speeds upward from as low as 3 mph.

The car was exported far and wide – even to the US – and assembled in Australia, Belgium, the UK, Ireland, South Africa and Spain. Its successor was the Renault Dauphine, introduced in 1956, although the 4CV continued in production until 1961.

RENAULT
1951
RENAULT A willing and tireless performer

SMILES, CONFIDENCE,
SPRIGHTLINESS, JOY OF LIVING...

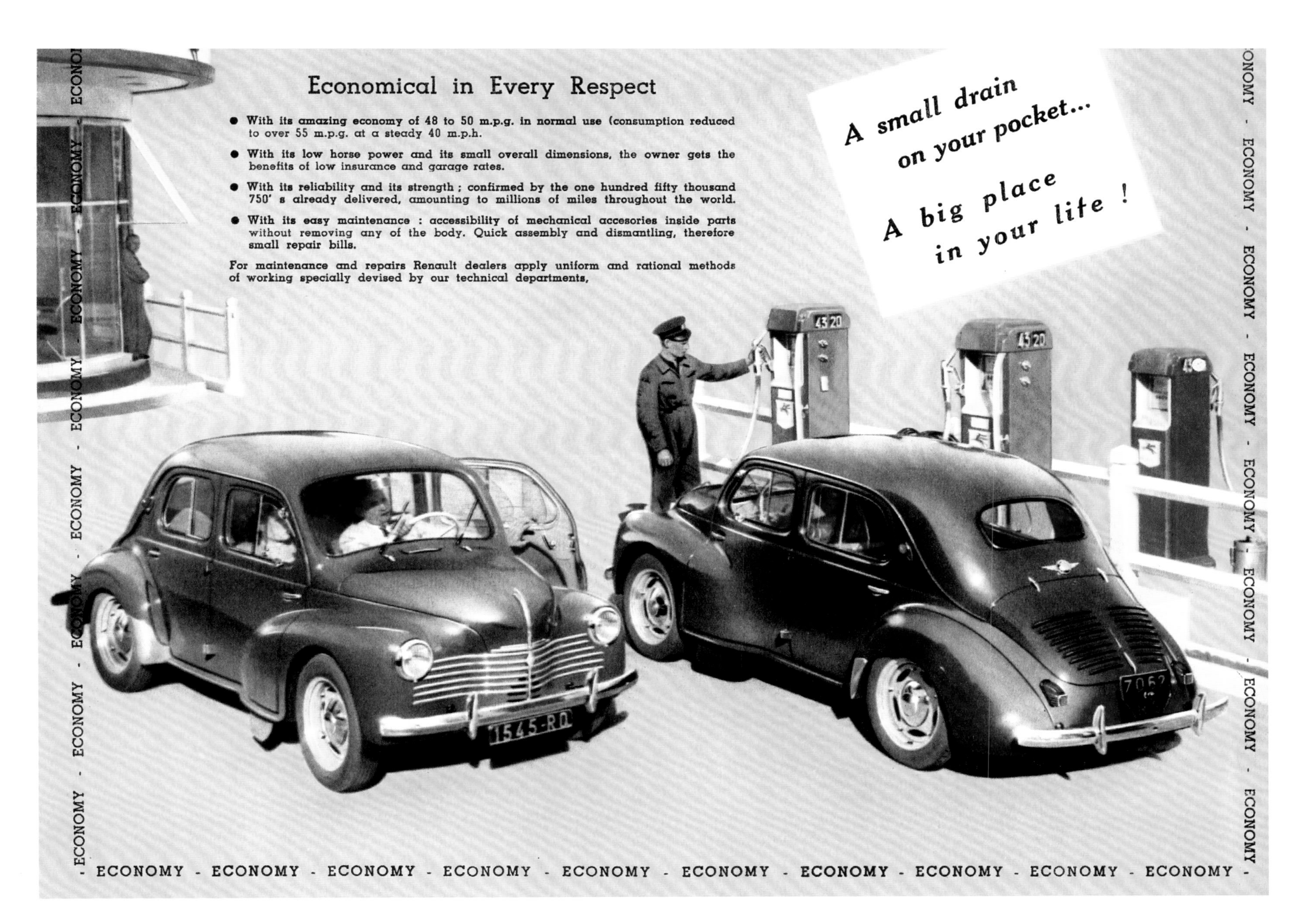

ABOVE The radiator cap – with distinctive art deco trim – was placed just above the engine compartment (as seen with the car at right above), and could easily be confused with the petrol cap, which was inside the engine compartment.

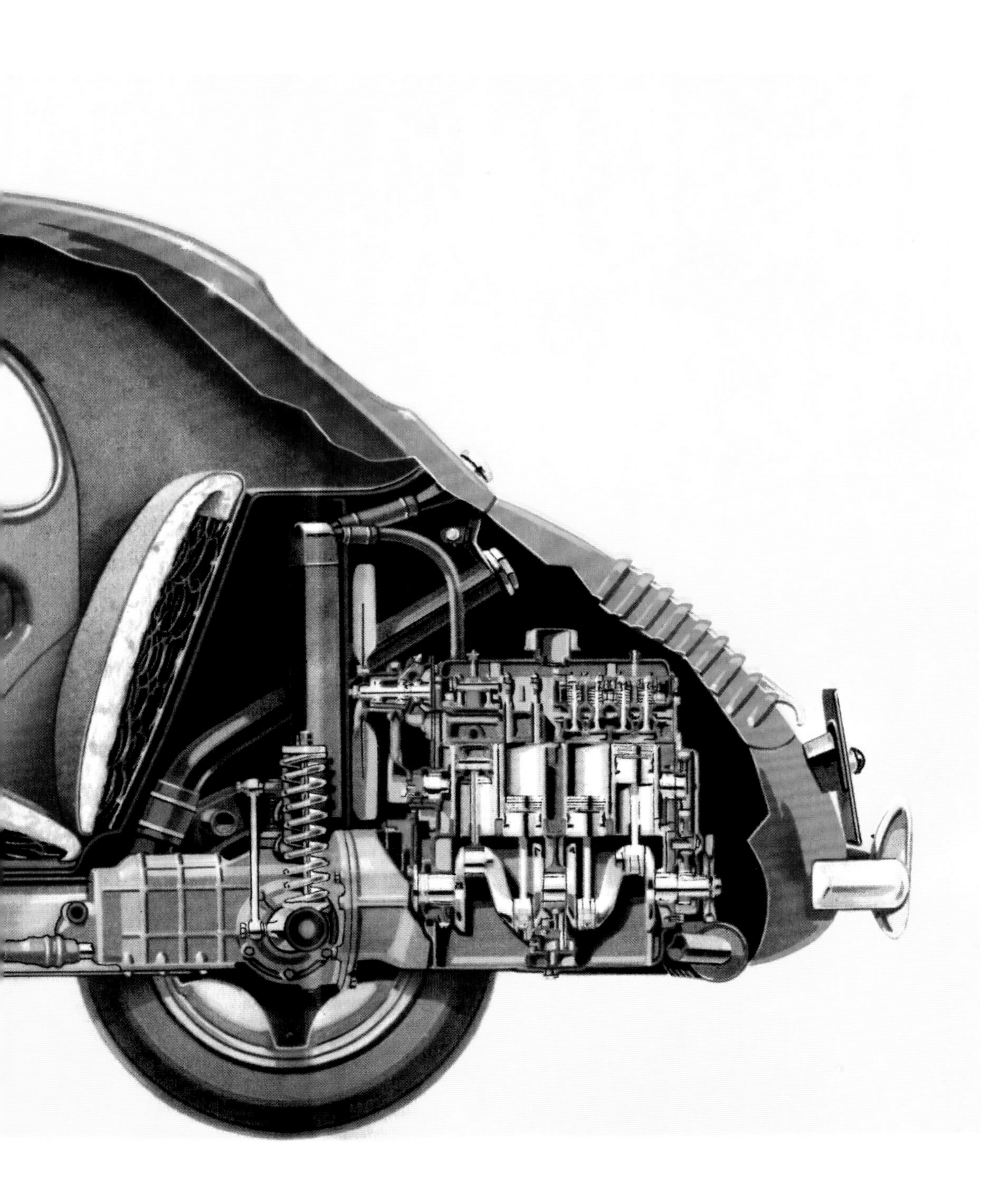

'Docile and flexible, driving a 750 is like walking or breathing – it comes naturally.'

ABOVE The spare wheel was stored up front.

LEFT The 4CV was just over 11 ft in length. The engine was set longitudinally in the rear.

AUSTIN A·70 HEREFORD

1948
Austin A70 Hereford

THE A70 HEREFORD AND ITS SISTER, THE A70 HAMPSHIRE, showed a similar styling to their A40 Devon predecessor (page 14) – but more rounded and characterful.

Austin's styling during the late 1940s and early 1950s was in the art deco mould, under the influence of lead designer Dick Burzi. The A70 models shared the trend towards ornate grilles and flowing lines, which started at the top of the car's front wings and swept down across the sides of the car, fading out past the rear doors.

The A70 Hampshire was introduced in 1948, and two years later it gave way to the 4-door A70 Hereford, now a little wider and a little longer. In addition, the range was expanded to include the 2-door Hereford convertible Coupe, Countryman estate and pick-up truck variants. Much of the Hampshire – including the doors and rear wings – had been borrowed from the Somerset, adding to the confusion in trying to identify Austins of the period. (A sure way to tell an A70 from an A40 is to look at the 'Austin of England' badges at the rear sides of the bonnet: those on the A70 incorporate a 'porthole' shape behind them, which is lacking on the A40.)

The Hereford Countryman was promoted as a versatile vehicle for both town and country: 'On the farm too, its sturdiness will prove equal to the many varied conditions of operation ... here is a model, dependable in the Austin tradition, combining the grace and good manners of a modern saloon car with the utility required by those who wish to carry goods.'

Power for the A70 came from the 2.2-litre 4-cylinder engine that had been used in the earlier Austin 16 hp car of 1945; top speed was over 80 mph. The A70's motor would go on to be used in the Austin A90 (page 50).

ABOVE A70 Hereford at Cains Motors in Silverstream, Upper Hutt, 1960s. An unusual configuration with its top-opening back and tailgate this Hereford was perhaps a special station-wagon model, or perhaps someone's post-purchase modification.

ABOVE Austins galore at Austin Motors, Dunedin, sometime in the early 1950s. At left is an attractive A70 Hampshire Countryman estate model with wood trim.

OPPOSITE The A70 Hereford. A distinguishing feature is the inset name badge just forward of the front window pillar.

Distinction and style in every line.

A profile of charm and dignity.

Luxurious riding comfort

'A peep through the windows of the A70 Hereford reveals an interior of quiet dignity that pleases the eye and invites closer acquaintance.'

Three adults can sit comfortably, with ample head- and leg-room, on the leather-trimmed Dunlopillo rear seat.

Excellent forward visibility for safe driving is afforded by the large-area, toughened, curved glass windscreen.

The ground clearance of the A70 ensures safe tra along rough tracks and corrugated up-country roa

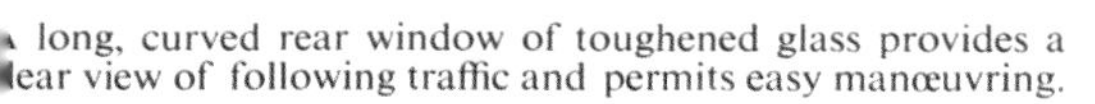
long, curved rear window of toughened glass provides a ear view of following traffic and permits easy manœuvring.

Wide, rear-opening doors with concealed hinges afford unobstructed ingress to and egress from the interior.

Generous luggage space is provided in the boot, while extra accommodation is obtained by lowering the lid.

*'In matters of estate
where distinguished service
is called for and where
adaptability is an important
factor, the A70 Countryman
takes pride of place.'*

OPPOSITE The A70 Hereford Pick-up. This shared the same platform as the Countryman estate, but with full bodywork fairing aft of the driving cab.

The bonnet can only be released from inside the cab. When in the raised position it permits easy access to the engine for routine maintenance.

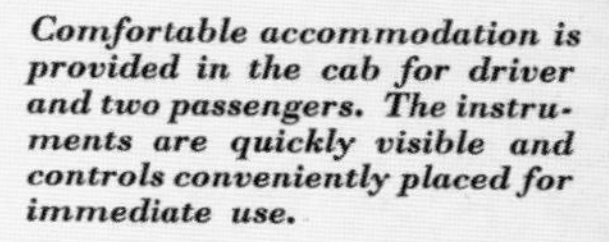

Comfortable accommodation is provided in the cab for driver and two passengers. The instruments are quickly visible and controls conveniently placed for immediate use.

The independent coil spring front suspension is controlled by double-acting hydraulic shock absorbers, and affords exceptionally smooth riding — even on the roughest surfaces.

A LIGHT OPEN TRUCK of 15-cwt. capacity, the Austin A70 Pick-Up has been specially developed to provide quick, economical and unfailing transport for those whose livelihood depends on the efficient delivery of goods and materials. Sturdily constructed, powerful and smooth in operation, the A70 Pick-Up can be relied on to give service first, service fast and dependable service always.

LAND
ROVER

1948
Land Rover

GREAT, GREAT VEHICLES. One wet day, while I was staying with friends up at Port Albert, I took their Series II out for a drive along their farm's tracks. All went well until, along one stretch, the Land Rover started slowly slipping sideways off the wet, slick clay camber, and it looked certain that vehicle and passengers would be delivered into the deepish drainage ditch alongside. At virtually the last moment, the four-wheel drive dug in and held, and the day was saved. The old Land Rovers may have been noisy and clunky on sealed surfaces, and not very fast, but they were – and still are – very cool, and the last word in get-you-home. They were also well liked. New Zealand is littered with old Land Rovers, a lot of them not in great condition, but people find it hard to get rid of them, such is their sentimental attachment.

First made in 1948, the Series Land Rovers were the original 4x4s. Influenced by the military Jeep, which had been such a visible part of the recently ended war, Land Rovers mirrored that vehicle's similar no-nonsense ethos. They were utilitarian, rugged and functional. There was nothing extraneous, no frills.

In the straitened post-war environment, the Rover company found itself in urgent need of a product that would fill the gap until car production could be fully resumed. It had to be built with materials that were readily available (steel was rationed), it had to secure export orders and it had to be manufactured quickly.

It was decided that the new vehicle should be very simple in design and styling, and that the bodywork should be in light alloy aluminium. This would reduce greatly the cost of tooling and, in turn, would shorten the pre-production time. The basic vehicle would have neither roof, doors nor windows. Further saving was made in the use of surplus aircraft cockpit paint (the various shades of light green sported by the early Land Rovers).

From the beginning, Rover saw the Land Rover as more than just a cross-country vehicle, and instead a vehicle that could do most of what a tractor did, and then get the farmer and his produce to market. Power take-off was integral to the Land Rover concept from 1948, enabling farm machinery and many other items to be run while the vehicle was stationary.

ABOVE Even to the ends of the earth: a Series II Land Rover at Scott Base in Antarctica during the 1954–55 season.

'All round the world, anywhere on earth in fact, four-wheel drive Land Rovers are doing work that no other vehicles can do. "Impossible" conditions have been overcome and "inaccessible" places reached by these ubiquitous machines whose unconquerable stamina and go-anywhere qualities have made them almost indispensable in many operational spheres.'

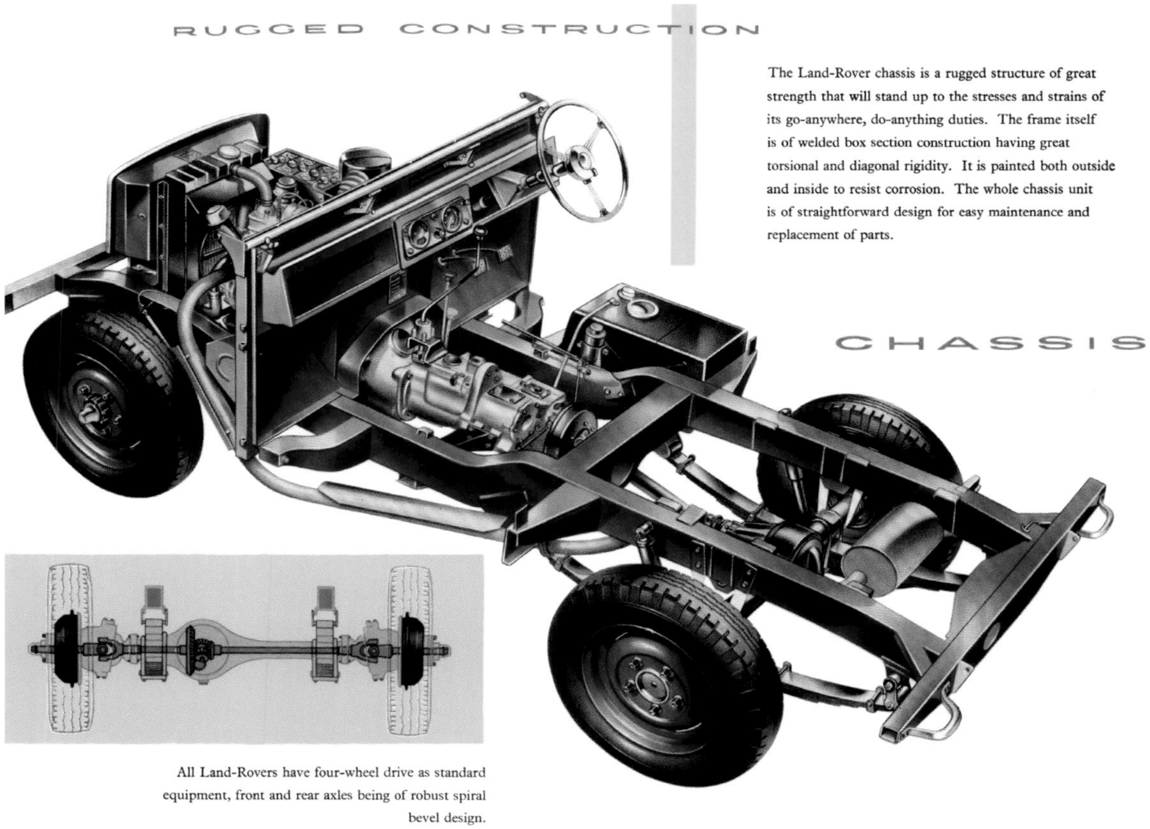

RUGGED CONSTRUCTION

The Land-Rover chassis is a rugged structure of great strength that will stand up to the stresses and strains of its go-anywhere, do-anything duties. The frame itself is of welded box section construction having great torsional and diagonal rigidity. It is painted both outside and inside to resist corrosion. The whole chassis unit is of straightforward design for easy maintenance and replacement of parts.

CHASSIS

All Land-Rovers have four-wheel drive as standard equipment, front and rear axles being of robust spiral bevel design.

ABOVE 1950 saw the advent of selectable (part-time) four-wheel drive (controlled by a third lever).

OPPOSITE Just as at home in the town as the countryside.

Evolution of the Land Rover quickened through the 1950s, the first year of that decade seeing the advent of selectable (part-time) four-wheel drive (controlled by a third lever on the central tunnel). In 1952, the engine size was increased to 1997 cc; 1957 saw the launch of Land Rover's first diesel engine; and in 1958 Rover introduced a Series II model with changes to the body styling. A new 2286 cc petrol engine was fitted in 1961 to create the Series IIA.

In 1971, the Land Rover appeared in Series III form. Further changes to the body styling saw headlights mounted in the front guards, not between them as previously. And, to the dismay of many people, gone was the original metal grille, replaced by a plastic one. The metal grille could be detached and used for cooking on, but sadly that was no longer possible.

The last of the old series Land Rovers was built in 1985, marking the end of what is probably the longest production run of any vehicle. During that time, two million Land Rovers were built.

LAND ROVER

88" WHEELBASE 'REGULAR'

The 88 in. wheelbase ' Regular,' four-wheel drive Land-Rover is the general factotum of the range, providing the sort of go-anywhere transport that is needed on farms, ranches, estates and indeed in any situation where versatility and cross-country mobility are required. It can operate as a completely open vehicle or be fully enclosed by the weather-proof canvas hood which is supplied as standard equipment. In either event the body provides excellent accommodation for three people and loads of up to 1,000 lb. (454 kg.).
All body panels are of non-rusting aluminium ; steel portions, such as hinges, handles and reinforcements being galvanised to resist corrosion. The vehicle is thus not affected by weather or climate and can work indefinitely under the most appalling conditions.
To add to its almost unlimited field of operation, the Land-Rover is provided with centre and rear power take-off points enabling many varied types of machinery to be driven.
All in all the Land-Rover can justly claim to be the world's most versatile vehicle.

In 1956, the wheelbase was increased by 2 inches to accommodate the Land Rover's first diesel engine.

88" WHEELBASE 'REGULAR' STATION WAGON

7 Seater version of the famous 4 wheel drive Land Rover

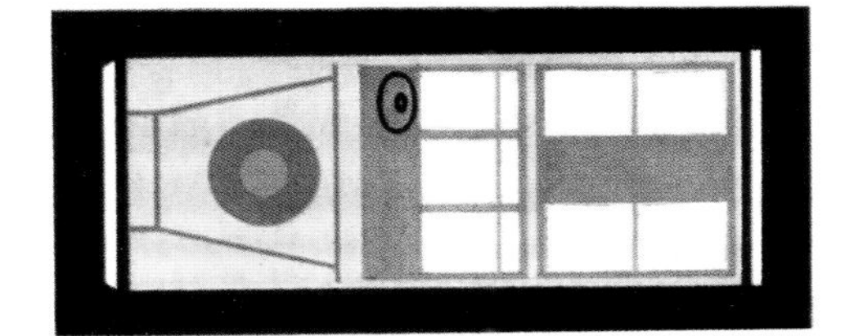

As an alternative passenger or goods carrier the Land-Rover 88 in. ' Regular ' Station Wagon has great appeal in territories where tough conditions are likely to be met. It will, for instance, travel smoothly and comfortably on made-up roads, deal easily with untended tracks, or with four-wheel drive engaged, take to the rough with a facility achieved by no other make of vehicle.

As a passenger carrier the Station Wagon is a seven seater. Accommodation is provided in the front compartment for three people, while four fold-up seats are fitted in the body, these being easily accessible through a wide door at the rear. With the seats folded, excellent floor space is available for the transport of goods and equipment of every kind.

Toughly built and having a generous ground clearance, the Land-Rover 88 in. wheelbase ' Regular ' Station Wagon is ever ready for day to day duty or high adventure in the inaccessible places of the world.

A large percentage of the Land Rover station wagons used in Africa (think Armand and Michaela Denis) were the long wheelbase models that could seat nine or more people and were set up with sturdy roof racks used as viewing or shooting platforms.

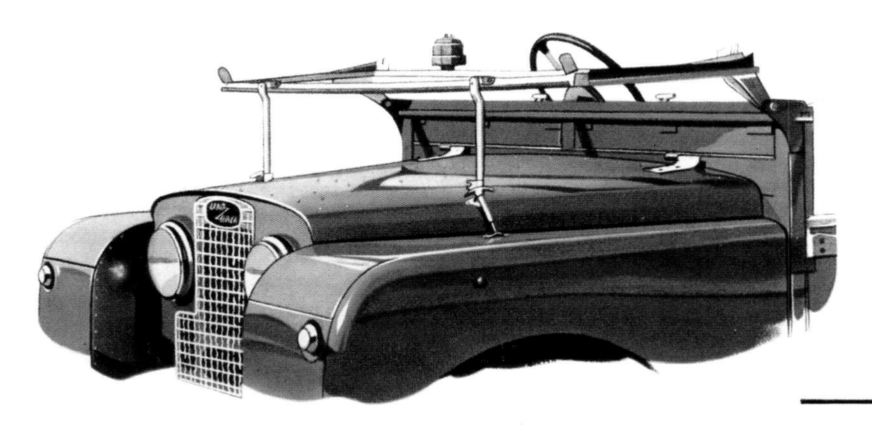

When required, the windscreen can be folded forward. It is held in this position by supports which are secured by the bonnet catch on each side.

Provision for carrying the spare wheel and tyre can be made either inside the body or on the bonnet, whichever is the more suitable position for the vehicle concerned or for the particular duties it has to perform.

Open Land-Rovers are provided with a tailboard which can be lowered into the horizontal position to facilitate loading and unloading.

The detachable hard-top has a lift-up type of door at the rear. With the vehicle tailboard lowered ample loading facilities are afforded.

A wide rear door and folding step give easy access to the rear seats of the Land-Rover Station Wagon. The door is lockable.

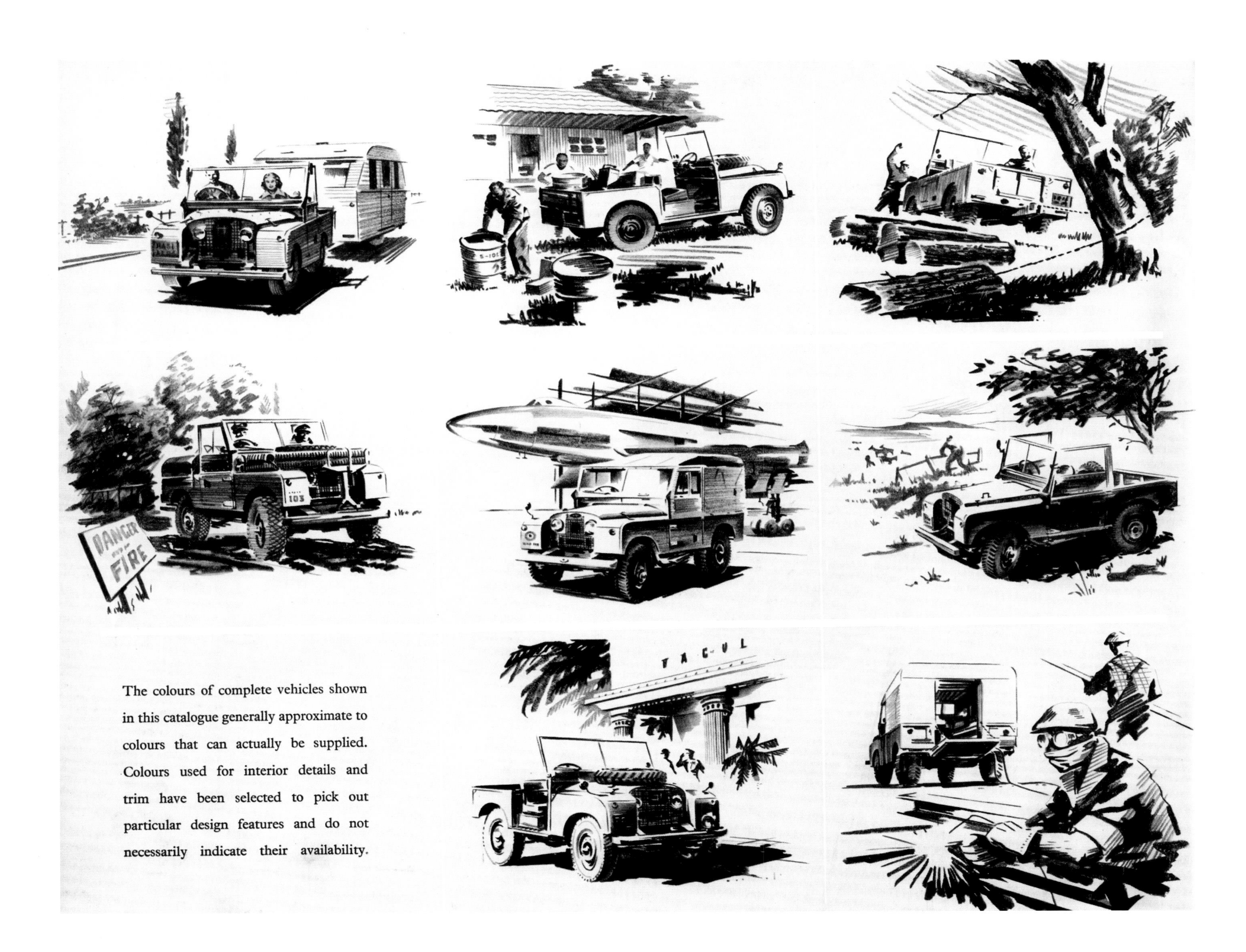

The colours of complete vehicles shown in this catalogue generally approximate to colours that can actually be supplied. Colours used for interior details and trim have been selected to pick out particular design features and do not necessarily indicate their availability.

1949

Austin A90 Atlantic

ABOVE Austin A90 Atlantic convertible taking part in racing at the Mairehau circuit, Canterbury, 1954.

LAUNCHED IN 1949, THE AUSTIN A90 ATLANTIC WAS AN ART DECO DELIGHT, with a Jaguaresque front treatment and quirky detailing. This included a third, centrally mounted main beam headlight, more famously used on the Rover 75 of the same year, resulting in that model being nicknamed 'Cyclops'. (The additional headlight idea didn't catch on for the Rover, and it was also discontinued in the A90 from 1952.)

Austin's intention with the A90 was a determined appeal to the lucrative American market for British sports cars, for which MG and others had established a demand. The A90 promised Hollywood styling, such as a wrap-around windscreen, spats on the rear wheels, powered windows and flashing turn indicators (replacing flag trafficators, which were more usual at the time). And, for added ventilation, the rear window could be wound down into the boot from the driver's seat. The chassis and running gear were based on those of Austin's A70 Hampshire (page 35), while power came from a beefed-up version of the A70's 2.6-litre 4-cylinder engine.

The car was launched as a 4-seat convertible, with a 2-door coupe version – the Atlantic A90 Sports Saloon – following in 1950. This model was offered with the options of a fixed-head roof – either painted or fabric-covered (to give the appearance of a convertible) – or a drophead cabriolet.

As part of promoting the car to the American market, Austin set new US motoring records using the A90. One car was driven continuously for seven days and nights at the Indianapolis Motor Speedway, covering more than 11,000 miles at an average speed in excess of 70 mph. In doing so, it broke dozens of records that until then had been held exclusively by American cars.

It appeared, however, that what the US market wanted when it came to car imports were British models that were styled differently to American cars, not ones trying to mimic them. They also wanted power, and while the A90's engine was big enough and provided speed enough for British buyers, it didn't compare with the existing V8-powered cars available to American motorists. Despite Austin's ambitious plans for the A90, only a few hundred ended up being exported to the US.

'Modern in every detail and designed for a brilliant performance, the A90 Atlantic Sports Saloon is a car of distinction that will bring an added zest to business or pleasure motoring. The gracefully styled four- or five-seater saloon body is a delight to the eye, and the attractive interior, softly upholstered, gives a high degree of passenger comfort.'

ABOVE The classier option for the Sports Saloon was a fabric-covered hood to provide the drophead cabriolet look. Both front wings on the A90 sported 'Flying A' ornaments; spats enclosed the rear wheels.

OPPOSITE The A90 was a determined tilt at the US market, but it turned out that potential American buyers wanted something more powerful and less 'American'.

Austin
'A 90' ATLANTIC
NEW today, famous tomorrow—here is the Austin 'A90' Atlantic Convertible providing, in the fullest measure, the finest motoring thrill of the age.
A galaxy of fine features includes the 88 h.p. overhead valve engine, steering column gear change, independent front wheel suspension, power or hand operated head and windows—and a low sweeping line which ensures full visibility and safe riding at all-out cruising speeds. Sunshine or rain, this new Austin gives the ride of a lifetime.
COLOURS AND TRIM

THE VOLKSWAGEN TRANSPORTER LINE

1949
Volkswagen Kombi

WHEN I WAS LIVING WITH FAMILY FRIENDS IN QUEENSTOWN FOR A TIME, it was my task once a month to do a supplies run. This involved driving my hosts' old split-screen Kombi first to the Invercargill meatworks, then on to Dunedin for mail and groceries, then back to Queenstown. It was a full day's drive, and when I eventually returned I remember it took a while before the vibration of hours of throbbing Volkswagen engine left me.

I also remember when I first drove the Kombi, how powerful it felt to sit right up at the front, immediately over the wheels, with *nothing* between me and the road ahead. The all-round visibility was terrific, like from the cockpit of a plane. Although noisy and not particularly fast, the Kombi was hugely enjoyable to drive.

Known as the Kombi (short for *Kombinationskraftwagen*, meaning 'combination motor vehicle') in New Zealand and Australia, and as the Microbus in a lot of other places, this was just one of the models produced in VW's Transporter series. It was introduced as VW's second car after the Beetle. Two models were on offer initially: the basic Kombi with side windows and middle and rear seats, and the Commercial. The first Kombis used the Beetle's 1100 cc, 24 hp motor (from 1953, the 1200 cc motor), an air-cooled flat, horizontally opposed 4-cylinder engine, mounted in the rear. It was not the most powerful of engines, and the key to its efficiency was in the gearing, by way of reduction gears at the ends of the swing axles.

A second-generation Kombi was released in 1967. Larger and heavier than the original, it no longer had a split windscreen but did boast a bigger, 1600 cc motor. The new Kombi also saw the old swing-axle arrangement replaced by half-axles with constant velocity joints.

In 1954, Jowett Motors in Auckland became the first VW-importer franchise in New Zealand; originally the vehicles arrived in built-up form, but later they were assembled at Jowett's plant in Otahuhu.

German production of the Kombi stopped after the 1967 model year; however, it continued to be made in Brazil in various forms until 1996.

ABOVE A VW Kombi being used as a school bus on a New Zealand country road sometime in the late 1950s. One of the early 'barn-door' Kombis with the high rear-engine door.

An original split-screen, 6-window Kombi pictured at Opawa, Christchurch, 1960s. During this decade you often came across the VW logo on the front turned into the symbol for universal peace/nuclear disarmament – particularly as opposition grew here to France's testing in the Pacific.

The back of the corner seat tilts forward to allow easy passage to the rear seats.

There are many ways of making or saving money; operating a Volkswagen Micro Bus is one of them, not only one of the best but also one of the safest. A bus — above all a Micro Bus — should be more than a mere means of low-cost transportation. Whoever travels in it should feel at ease and enjoy the ride. Both the Volkswagen Micro Bus and the even smarter "De Luxe" provide that amount of comfort which can be rightly expected by a passenger; both give that degree of economy which will be required by their owner.

The double side doors, wide-opening and of generous width, give easy access to the spacious interior. Roomy upholstered seats with soft, deeply sprung cushions and backrests ensure a comfortable ride. The luggage is loaded through the rear into the separate spacious luggage compartment which holds about 16 average-size suitcases and is completely out of the way of passengers.

Bright windows of safety glass give full vision all round. One of the most difficult problems — air conditioning — has been effectively solved by the adjustable, roof-mounted ventilation system, by outward-opening, pivoting and sliding windows, thus doing justice to even the most sensitive passenger. And when it gets cold, an efficient heater is turned on to spread comfortable warmth.

The well balanced front and rear wheel suspension is designed not only to ensure quiet running of the vehicle but also to convey that feeling of perfect security so highly appreciated by every Volkswagen passenger.

A good initial investment, the Volkswagen Micro Bus quickly turns out to be a major asset to its owner, for he will soon find out that it does as much as 30 m.p.g. (Imp.) — 25 m.p.g. (U.S.), 9.5 litres/100 kilometers, carrying as many as eight passengers; his own experience will soon show that it hardly needs any repairs even after having been driven 60,000 miles or more. Finally, he need no longer worry whether his bus will return safely from a tour, for he knows the ease and safety with which the Micro Bus moves even in the densest traffic.

In fact, there is nothing like the Volkswagen Micro Bus, whatever standards you may apply.

While the passengers are entering through the wide double doors, the driver or a porter is able to stow their baggage, without inconvenience to them, in the large luggage compartment in the rear.

Early models, until around 1955, were sometimes called 'barn-door' Kombis in reference to the high rear-engine door. The shelf above the engine was a disadvantage when it came to loading, as the engine cover intruded on the interior space.

Volkswagen Transporters
for every job
in every line of business

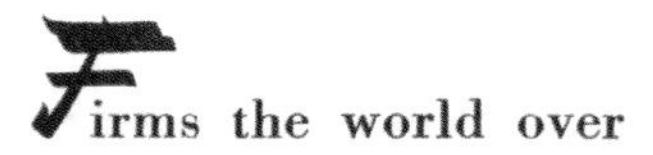

Firms the world over

have long needed economical light-duty trucks perfectly fitted for the job at hand

so that delivery costs can be drastically reduced.

Following closely the advice of users of light-duty trucks,

Volkswagen engineers have designed a line of commercial models

that fill this need to perfection.

Volkswagen Transporters

—a model for every type of job—

offer you more than you ever dreamed of.

Nearly 100,000 of them are already in service.

ABOVE Adaptable in so many ways, VW Transporters were the epitome of practical transport.

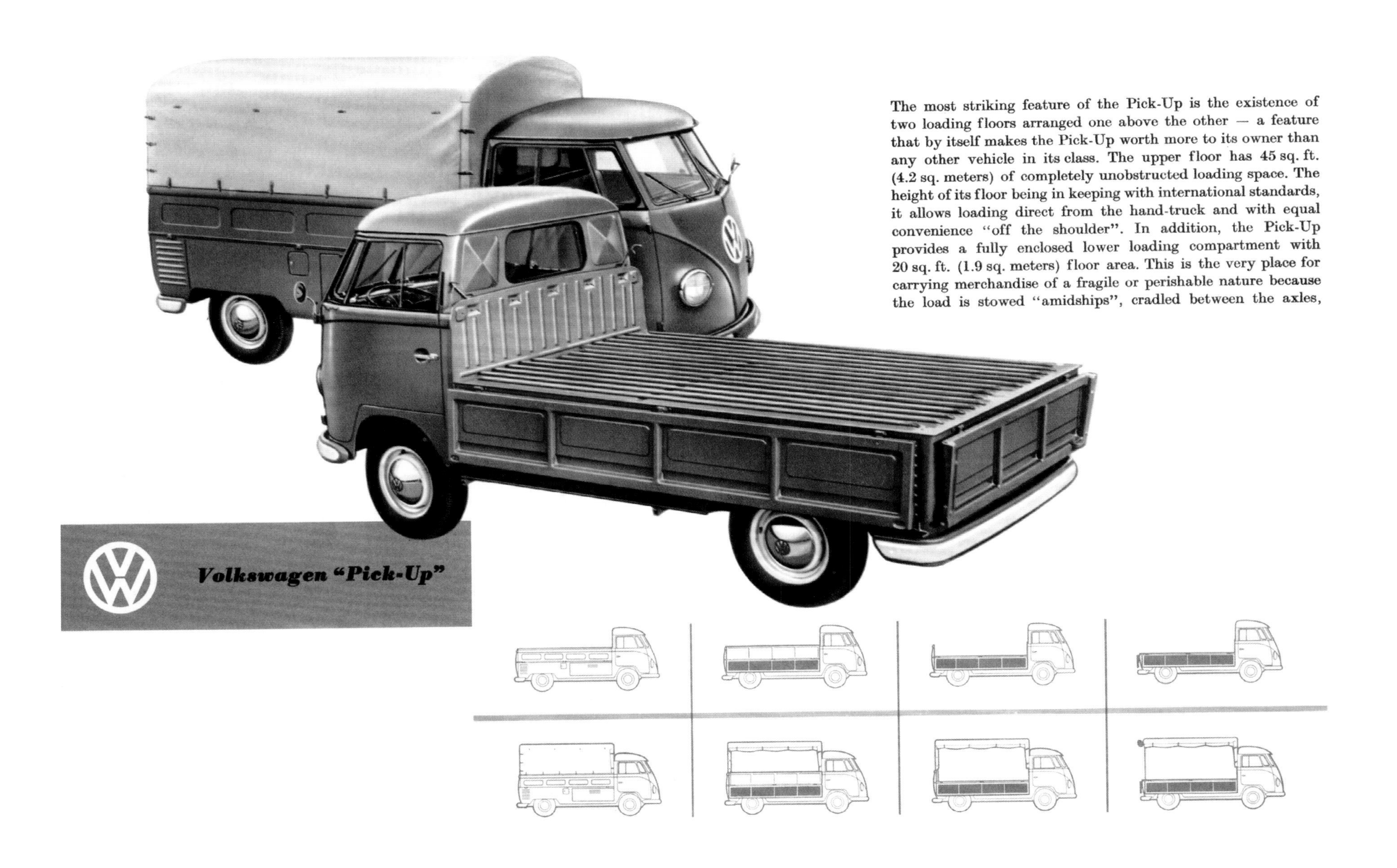

The most striking feature of the Pick-Up is the existence of two loading floors arranged one above the other — a feature that by itself makes the Pick-Up worth more to its owner than any other vehicle in its class. The upper floor has 45 sq. ft. (4.2 sq. meters) of completely unobstructed loading space. The height of its floor being in keeping with international standards, it allows loading direct from the hand-truck and with equal convenience "off the shoulder". In addition, the Pick-Up provides a fully enclosed lower loading compartment with 20 sq. ft. (1.9 sq. meters) floor area. This is the very place for carrying merchandise of a fragile or perishable nature because the load is stowed "amidships", cradled between the axles,

The new AUSTIN A40 Somerset
AUS 40

1952 Austin A40 Somerset

MORE STYLISH THAN ITS A40 DEVON (PAGE 14) AND A70 HEREFORD (PAGE 34) PREDECESSORS, the Somerset had a new front-end design that included a more attractive grille. It was also more Rubenesque: rounded, flowing lines swirled aft from the top of the front wings to the rear wheels. Similar in size to the Devon, the Somerset used the same running gear as that model and had a similar top speed of around 70 mph. A 2-door convertible followed after the release of the 4-door saloon.

The Somerset's interior held two close-fitting, leather-upholstered front seats capable of being set together to form a bench seat. In the back was a deeply cushioned bench seat for three. The car had a symmetrical arrangement, with gloveboxes for the front passenger and driver each side of centrally positioned gauges; this configuration making it a simple matter for the factory to produce both right- and left-hand-drive versions of the car.

The car was a somewhat stolid drive, part of the explanation for this lying (as with other British cars of the war and immediate post-war periods) with the poor petrol quality available, which necessitated retarded ignition settings to prevent the engine knocking or 'pinking'. When standard octane petrol became available at the pump once more, Somerset owners could purchase from Austin a replacement distributor and a thinner head gasket to alter the ignition settings, thereby helping raise compression and improving performance.

The handling of many British cars of the period demonstrated a soft lean through corners. And that was in new vehicles. In older, used cars, the suspension only got worse. The A40 in particular seemed to suffer in this department, and driving the Somerset was compared to by one writer as driving a 'spongy pud'. (Such negative qualities in cars of the time only helped improve our car-handling skills, however.) Drivers of vehicles whose lever-arm shock absorbers were very badly worn might find their car bouncing and wobbling on its suspension for a time after it had come to a halt.

The Somerset ended its run in 1954, when it was replaced by the A40 Cambridge.

ABOVE An A40 Somerset parked opposite the Avoncourt Hotel on the corner of Great North Road (foreground) and Wingate Street, Auckland.

The new AUSTIN A4

WHETHER you enjoy motoring for its own sake or whether business dictates your journeying, you will derive infinite pleasure from the handsome A40 Somerset.

Based on a chassis that has given to motorists everywhere a fuller appreciation of light car travel it is enthusiastically welcomed as a brilliant addition to a famous range of cars. Its performance is outstanding, for it will crawl unfalteringly with slow-moving traffic, yet at a touch of the accelerator will spring to life with a surge of power that speeds it well into the upper 60's. In comfort too it is right at the top of its class with a tastefully planned interior and comfortable foam rubber seating covered in real leather.

These great qualities, combined with economy in operation and ease of control, ensure for the A40 Somerset supreme success both at home and overseas.

Convenience of controls, dignity in design and clear all-round vision are featured in the A40 Somerset saloon. Note also the close-mounted individually adjustable front seats and generous leg room.

Somerset

THE
AUS 40

The A40 Somerset Convertible. The 'Flying A' ornament fitted to the top front of Austin bonnets of this period has to have been one of the best car manufacturer motifs ever produced. On the A40 Somerset, it incorporated the bonnet release. The Somerset Convertible had the option of an elegant coupe configuration (above) if you didn't want to lower the roof all the way back.

1953
Ford Prefect 100E

ABOVE Ford Prefect on the forecourt of the Cranford Street Shell Service Station, Christchurch, 1969. This looks to be a 107E model that came with extra chrome on the front guards, and tended to have a two-tone exterior.

FORD UK'S MOVE TO UNITARY CONSTRUCTION, first used with the Zephyr/Zodiac of 1951, continued on the company's new 100E range of small cars launched in 1953. Moving away from the old upright style of car to a lower modern design, the new Prefect and Anglia – and eventually also the replacement Popular – were basic, easily maintained and enjoyable to drive. They were robust little cars and gave good service. A new side-valve 1172 cc engine was fitted, capable of powering the cars to a top speed of about 70 mph.

The 100E was made in a basic 2-door Anglia form and as the higher-specced Prefect, which had four doors and vertical bars on the radiator grille (as distinct from the Anglia's horizontal bars). De Luxe versions were also produced. When the Anglia 105E was launched in 1959, the Anglia 100E became the Popular 100E, a low-budget, bottom-of-the-range vehicle aimed at competing on price with the British Motor Corporation's new Mini.

A variant of the Prefect, the 107E, was introduced in 1959. This used a reworked 100E body with the 997 cc overhead-valve engine from the new Anglia 105E, optional two-tone colour schemes plus deluxe trim in the form of extra chrome work. Other additions included a radio and leather upholstery to replace the standard vinyl. A test car recorded a top speed of 73 mph. Versions assembled in New Zealand at Ford's Seaview plant came with a heater and carpet.

The last of the 100Es was made in 1963.

The car that steps up 10 h.p. motoring
to all-better standards
PREFECT

All-round visibility

Curved windscreen and rear window give better visibility than in any other car in its class. You are safer in the hands of Ford.

PREFECT De Luxe

ABOVE Ford's new 'family' styling strategy saw the Prefect, Anglia and Popular models turned out in scaled-down Consul–Zephyr form.

RIGHT The Prefect dashboard went through a number of facelifts from its original form here, showing dials within a binnacle surrounding the steering column. A 1959 revision added a 'magic ribbon' speedo of the kind used with the Vauxhall 1958–59 PA models.

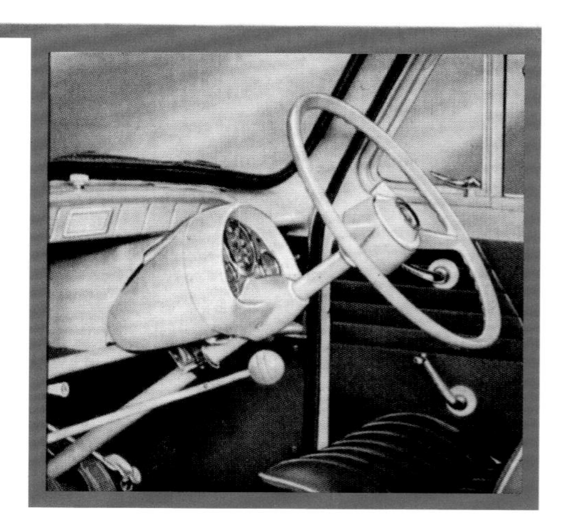

Prefect De Luxe - A New Ford 5-Star Car

Loads of Room

The large boot is a favourite feature in the Prefect. 10 cu. ft. await to be filled.

This will be the first sight the family see of your new Prefect De Luxe when it comes sweetly down the road and into your garage.
The chrome will be sparkling—everything will be as fresh and as exciting as new paint.
You can't help admiring the skilfully styled headlights and radiator.

Instrument panel

Hand controls and instruments have been regrouped in the De Luxe instrument panel.

Open any of the 4 doors and you see how roomy it is in front and especially at the back. Then step in and try the seats for comfort. There is a new softness to make any journey a pleasure. You can choose your own upholstery from a wide range of plain and contemporary patterns.

Foot controls

The pendant pedals are designed to eliminate draughts. Clutch and brakes are hydraulically operated. Large brake drums ensure maximum safety.

FORD MOTOR COMPANY LTD

DAGENHAM

PREFECT De Luxe

It's a beautiful car. Neat and sturdy with plenty of Ford 'go'.
It reflects all that is best in modern car design.
New features on the Prefect De Luxe and twin wing mirrors give added ease and safety to driving. They also give this elegant car a jaunty look.
Chrome window surrounds add a touch of luxury.
The chrome body strip is a bright, elegant addition to your Prefect De Luxe.
And what about the engine? It is a 1172 cc. power unit that has already proved itself over millions of miles. Ford running economy goes without saying —and, of course, Ford Service too.

PREFECT

The Prefect gives a valiant service to many families who want a car with plenty of room, plenty of 'go' and an economical performance.
Headroom,legroom and all-round visibility leave nothing to be desired. Differing in several external and internal details, the Prefect is basically identical to the De Luxe version.
Power unit, gearbox and sturdy all-steel body have been designed to give long life reliability.
Many people who can afford more expensive cars run a Prefect. That is strong proof of its success in all walks of life.

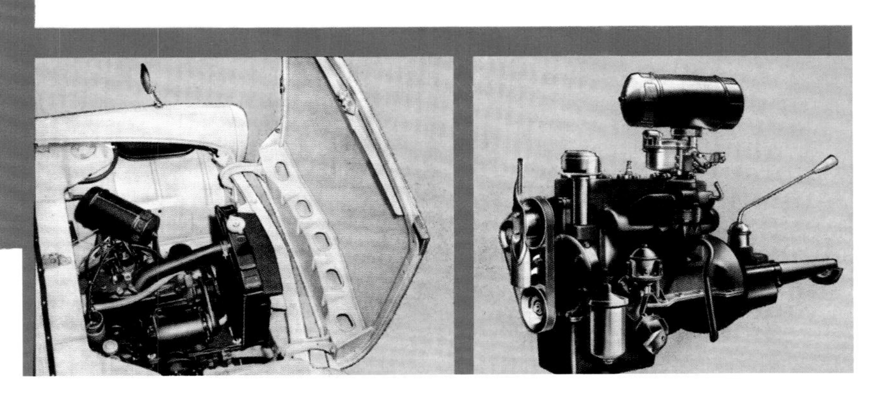

PUBLICATION No. H. & E. 5752
MG
MAGNETTE
ONE AND A HALF LITRE SALOON
UWL 546

1953
MG Magnette ZA & ZB

IT MAY HAVE BEEN SPORTIER TO LOOK AT THAN TO DRIVE, but the MG Magnette was one of those cars that got to you, especially when many British cars of the time appeared so staid in their narrow, upright styling. By comparison, the Magnette – designed by Gerald Palmer, who was also responsible for the lovely Jowett Javelin (page 20) – was a sleeker and more attractively proportioned car. It shared the same bodyshell as the Wolseley 4/44 (when the Nuffield Group became part of the British Motor Corporation, MG also became part of BMC's strategy of maximising sales by badge engineering), but it was far more sporty looking and handled better, thanks to its lower stance (the MG was some 2 inches lower than the Wolseley). Its curved grille added further distinction.

The Magnette was produced in ZA and ZB models between 1952 and 1958. A second-build series of a Mk III and Mk IV MG Magnette followed (1959 through 1968), also utilising Wolseley bodies.

The more powerful ZB variant replaced the ZA in 1956, and was offered with optional 'Varitone' two-colour paintwork and a wrap-around rear screen. Power was increased to 64 hp, giving a top speed of 86 mph.

Later ZBs had the option of a clutchless, semi-automatic transmission called Manumatic. This was an advanced system powered by vacuum from the inlet manifold and operated by a unique clutch assembly that was activated by the gear knob rather than depressing a clutch pedal: 'Manumatic gear change is now offered on the MG Magnette as an optional extra. Gears are selected merely by movement of the gear lever. The clutch is automatically engaged and disengaged, thus leaving only the brake and accelerator pedals to be operated by foot.'

A Mk III Magnette came out in 1959 (updated as a Mk IV in 1961) in the mould of BMC's Farina-designed, mid-sized saloon line. Here, the Magnette suffered the indignity of losing its individuality among members of a badge-engineered family that also included the very similar-looking Riley, Austin, Morris Oxford and Wolseley. Gone was the complete charm of the ZA and ZB cars.

ZA and ZB Magnettes were mostly imported to New Zealand already built up.

ABOVE MG Magnette ZA, pictured at the Caltex Waihi service station, late 1950s.

'When you catch a glimpse of your friends in the driving mirror ... overhear an envious phrase ... sense their glow of admiration, then you will be prouder still, as a man of moderate means, to be the owner of this luxury class car.'

'Loath though a man is to face the fact, there comes a point in the sports car enthusiast's life when the children have grown just too big to fit in the luggage compartment of the "sports" ... you must become, you hesitate to utter the word, an ordinary "saloon" car owner. But wait – what was it you heard about the MG Magnette?'

THE NEW *airsmoo*

ABOVE They weren't the fastest of sporting saloons, but the ZA and ZB Magnettes did offer some real style and excellent road-holding.

ed

MAGNETTE SALOON (SERIES "ZA")

LOATH though a man is to face the fact, there comes a point in the sports car enthusiast's life when the children have grown just too big to fit in the luggage compartment of " the sports " . . . when the wife is a little less keen on the wind whistling through her hair . . . when your business position requires a car with a somewhat more refined exhaust noise. A sad moment indeed, you think ; a moment to pause and look back over many happy years of club competitions, of rallies and of countless little " dices " which you have enjoyed on the open road. That is all over, you sigh ; you must become, you hesitate to utter the word, an ordinary " saloon " car owner. But wait—what was it you heard about the M.G. Magnette ? No ordinary saloon car . . . a powerful sporting engine . . . graceful body styling . . . crisp, traffic-beating acceleration . . . luxuriously finished interior . . . meticulously planned driving position . . . wide, uninterrupted vision. Yes, this is the car for you ; and the wife ; and the children. You are not ejected from the sporting fraternity after all ; you are promoted—promoted to a new high level of " Comfort with Performance " " Safety Fast " motoring.

GOES LIKE THE WIND . . . AND smoothly!

ABOVE The lovely drawing-room feel of the Magnette cabin. Front and rear seats were leather-trimmed, while the dash and door cappings were of polished wood.

RIGHT The option of Varitone two-tone paintwork was offered with the advent of the ZB model.

OPPOSITE The ZA signalled the first appearance of MG's new 4-cylinder 1.5-litre B-Series engine. Aided by twin SU carburettors, the motor generated 60 bhp, power enough for a top speed of 80 mph.

ELEGANCE THROUGHOUT

From every point of view the M.G. Magnette is a good-looking car. The elegance of its airsmoothed line is matched by the all-round excellence of its interior finish. Deep, comfortable seats are upholstered in best English leather—unsurpassed for appearance and enduring quality—non-wearing parts in leathercloth. The craftsman-built facia panel and handsome door cappings are in beautifully grained polished walnut, whilst floor carpet adds the final touch of luxury.

A duo-tone Magnette, which has also a large wrap-round rear window, is available.

DUO-TONE SCHEMES FOR THE MAGNETTE

Steel Blue with Maroon or Black upholstery

Twilight Grey with Grey or Maroon upholstery

TOP BODY COLOUR	LOWER BODY COLOUR	UPHOLSTERY
Island Green	Reseda Green	Green or Black
Steel Blue	Mineral Blue	Grey or Black
Ivory	Autumn Red	Maroon or Biscuit
Birch Grey	Twilight Grey	Maroon
Island Green	Black	Green
Steel Blue	Black	Maroon
Ivory	Black	Maroon
Birch Grey	Black	Maroon

Lively and flexible, the M.G. Magnette is equally at home in town or country. With maximum fuel economy the superb new engine supplies power a-plenty with remarkable flexibility of performance. Carefully planned gear and power-to-weight ratios ensure excellent acceleration and effortless climbing. At an engine speed of 5,400 *r.p.m. it develops* 68 *b.h.p. This power is achieved with a comparatively short stroke, which means brisker acceleration.*

1953
Nash Metropolitan

'The Metropolitan combines polo-pony nimbleness in traffic with superb comfort ... You who like sports-car dash and verve will, of course, be captivated by the Metropolitan.'

LOOKING UNNERVINGLY LIKE A FAIRGROUND DODGEM CAR, with its dinky boat-shaped body and pastel paintwork, the Metropolitan was surely from a comic book. It was a curiosity and just seemed so ... *unlikely*.

Views on the Metropolitan's performance were mixed. Described by one writer as 'a fleet, sporty little bucket which should prove just what the doctor ordered for a second car' and a 'nice-handling car with plenty of control and amazing dig, considering it is powered by a small Austin A-40 engine', driving the Metropolitan was said by another commentator to be 'like a yacht in a storm'. The short wheelbase certainly made for erratic handling on rough roads, although its low centre of gravity and good weight distribution did make it fun to drive.

It was the Nash company's intention to launch the Metropolitan in the American market to satisfy what it saw as a demand for a small, economical, city commuter car – a car that was inexpensive, compact and peppy. To achieve the first of these ambitions, and in the face of prohibitive tooling costs in the US, Nash decided to outsource manufacturing to the UK. They contracted the Austin Motor Company to build the car using existing Austin components (engine, suspension, transmission and electrical systems, and brakes), leaving tooling costs confined to the body panels only.

The Metropolitan was sold as both a convertible and a hard-top. It was very small – smaller than the Volkswagen Beetle – and could have been a little more practical. Up until 1960, when the bodyshell eventually incorporated an opening boot, the rear storage compartment could be accessed only by leaning the rear-seat forward and reaching back.

The first models used Austin's 1200 cc straight-four engine (as used in the A40 Devon, page 14), which in the Series II Metropolitan was changed for the B-Series motor, also 1200 cc. Top speed was around 70 mph.

In 1955, a revamped model – the Series III – made its appearance. The engine capacity was increased to 1498 cc, and American Motors (as Nash had become) gave it the designation 'Metropolitan 1500' to differentiate it from the earlier 1200 cc model.

Metropolitan "1500"

"Luxury in Miniature"

Nash was aiming the Metropolitan at the two-car family, as a second car for women or an economical commuter car.

A cosmetic change saw stainless-steel trims incorporated into the sides of the body, which allowed for the option of two-tone paintwork. Duo-toning had the effect of lengthening and lowering the look of the car. A major redesign saw the launch of the Series IV model in 1959, which included – finally – the addition of a boot lid.

Although satisfactory, sales of the Metropolitan in the US never increased beyond the initial sales levels – Americans may have wanted economy and even compactness in theory, but in reality, it seems they found it difficult to give up their preoccupations with size and speed.

METROPOLITAN "1500" HARDTOP COUPE

It took Nash to do it!

Everybody's talked about it . . . about the need and place in America for a car engineered from the *wheels up* to combine the superb performance, comfort and economy demanded in a family car with the dash and roadability of a sportster.

Yes — everybody's talked about it for years — but it took Nash to do it!

And here it is . . . the Metropolitan . . . the result of 11 years of Nash engineering research . . . a car that thousands of Americans who previewed our experimental models helped design.

It's a handsome, head-turning car — 149½ inches of breath-taking, compact new beauty. It's a he-man car, a car that hustles up steepest hills, over roughest roads, and rides with unbelievable smoothness.

The Metropolitan is completely different from any car you have known. It was born of our conviction that there is a need in America for a low-priced yet fine, shorter wheelbase car, luxuriously finished and precision-built, engineered to today's driving needs.

The Metropolitan is backed by one of the world's great industrial organizations — Nash Motors — with research and engineering "know-how" second to none.

The Metropolitan is another major milestone in the trailblazing tradition of Nash. It is the latest of a long line of Nash "FIRSTS" dating back to 1902 when the "granddaddy" of all Nash cars, the original Rambler — one of America's first mass-produced automobiles — was introduced.

Facts About

The Metropolitan. The name was just about longer than the car. The new Metropolitan was made in two body designs: convertible and hard-top. It was later sold under the Hudson name when Nash–Kelvinator and Hudson merged in 1954 to form the American Motors Corporation, and later still under its own name.

Exciting New

olitan

Up to 40 Miles to the Gallon

Unbelievably Low Operating Costs

Two Custom Models – Convertible and Hardtop

Advanced Nash Styling on a new, exciting scale.

Luxurious custom-tailored interiors that set a new standard in quality for cars of this size

Amazing Riding Comfort

Custom Appointments and Equipment for your complete motoring pleasure.

The Metropolitan "1500"

MEET THE WORLD'S SMARTEST SMALLER CAR! **The Metropolitan "1500" provides smart, sound, sensible transportation for two people plus, in either of two distinctive body styles—Hardtop Coupe and dashing Convertible. You'll like the sparkling, yet thrifty power . . . the sensational handling ease in traffic . . . the responsiveness on the open road. Here, truly, is luxury in miniature . . . "A watch-charm Rolls-Royce" as Devon Francis described the Metropolitan in Popular Science Monthly.**

METROPOLITAN "1500"™ CONVERTIBLE

In 1956, Austin Motors did a deal with American Motors that allowed it to sell Series III and IV Metropolitans in those countries where the latter didn't have a presence.

Rover 90

1953
Rover 90

THIS ALWAYS SEEMED ONE OF THE CLASSIEST OF THE OLD CARS: stately and understated. In the 1950s, Rover was a manufacturer of quality mid-sized luxury saloon cars. Beautifully made, they were built to last. Look closely at these cars today, and you soon see how very good they were and still are, combining high design, quality build, strong engines and comfortable, luxurious interiors of leather upholstery and wood trim: 'Refinement is quickly apparent in the quiet dignity of Rover coachwork. The interior is roomy, beautifully equipped ... An added air of distinction is given by the fascia and window frames, which are finished in selected walnut.'

In 1949, the company released the first P4 series models. The line would run until 1964 and included a range of models with increasingly powerful engines and greater refinements. The first of these was the 6-cylinder Rover 75, famous for its third 'Cyclops' headlight set between the two main driving lights. The range then evolved through the 4-cylinder Rover 60 (1953), the top-end 6-cylinder Rover 90 (also 1953), and the later Rover 100 and 110.

The Rover 90 was the most successful and ubiquitous of these. Refined yet strong, it had a 2.6-litre engine that allowed an easily achieved top speed of 90 mph. The motoring correspondent of *The Times* wrote, 'At a time when Britain's leading position in world markets is being increasingly challenged by Continental and American motor manufacturers it is a reassuring experience to drive the River 90 saloon.'

The Rover 90 was replaced in 1959 by the Rover 100, with the final P4 models – the 95 and the last of the line, the 110 – introduced in 1962. These later models added power-assisted steering and overdrive (early P4 Rovers, which lacked overdrive, were fitted with a freewheel clutch that allowed the engine to run more economically and also enabled the driver to change gears without using the clutch; the freewheel clutch was dropped in 1959 when overdrive became available).

By now, however, the P4 styling was beginning to look increasingly dated. After 15 years, it was time for Rover to bring in a more modern look, which it did in groundbreaking fashion with the Rover 2000 of 1963.

OPPOSITE 'The Ninety is a luxury car by any classification and combines an outstanding performance with supreme comfort and impressive smoothness and silence ... at 50 mph the most obtrusive sound is the ticking of the clock.'

The Ninety is a luxury car by any classification and combines an outstanding performance with supreme comfort and impressive smoothness and silence. Even when travelling at maximum speed passengers may relax in the well-furnished interior and talk in normal tones. Power is provided by a six-cylinder engine of 2,638 c.c. capacity developing 93 brake horse-power and operating with commendable economy. This economy may be further improved by the fitting of automatic overdrive which is available as an optional extra.

ABOVE The unusual gear shift was designed so that, with three people in the front, its operation was out of their way.

LEFT The Rover 90's bodyshell used aluminium panels for the doors, bonnet and boot lid; with the introduction of the 95 and 110 models, this was substituted with steel. The P4 Rovers were among the last British cars to have so-called 'suicide doors' – the back doors hinged on the rear edge. As luxurious as the 90 was, it wasn't quite as limousine-like as the brochure's artist rendered it in this illustration.

Another admirable feature of Rover detail design is the sliding tool tray fitted beneath the fascia parcel compartment. It provides a most sensible and secure method of stowing the small hand tools with which the car is issued.

1955
Volkswagen Karmann Ghia

THE KARMANN GHIA WAS ANOTHER CAR MUCH ADMIRED but something of a rarity in New Zealand. This was mainly for reasons of price (the cars were comparatively expensive here for what you got) and performance, which did not quite match those exotic looks. Using the same engine as the Volkswagen Beetle, which had been designed for the less-demanding topography of central Europe, the Karmann Ghia could have done with a more powerful engine when it came to driving our steeper and more winding roads (the original 1192 cc motor was subsequently increased in capacity to 1584 cc).

Beneath its skin, the Karmann Ghia (which was styled by the Italian design company Ghia and had bodywork by German coachbuilder Karmann) was a plain VW Beetle – given the Beetle's simple floor pan, it was comparatively easy to build special bodies to fit.

First sold in 1955 as a coupe, the Karmann Ghia was also produced in convertible form a couple of years later. In 1962, Volkswagen launched a restyled, more razor-edged design, the 1500 Karmann Ghia. This featured a new, flat 1500 cc motor capable of pushing the car to a top speed of 90 mph. (VW engines were built so precisely that you could get into a Ghia and drive at top speed right from the start. This was in contrast to most British cars of the time, which required a period of 'running in', as often advised by a handwritten note to the effect in the back window with the request to 'please pass'.)

The 1500 delivered not only greater performance than its predecessor but was also more spacious and accessorised. A sliding steel sunroof was offered as an option. An alternative to the Karmann Ghia coupe was the Touring Coupe, introduced in 1970 and fitted with VW's 1584 cc flat-four air-cooled boxer motor unit, as used in the Variant.

A total of 445,000 Karmann Ghias were turned out over the car's run, from 1955 to 1974.

ABOVE VW Karmann Ghia on display at the Shelly Motors stand at an A&P Show in the Hutt Valley, 1960s.

'The secret of the Karmann Ghia's beauty lies in its simplicity. Each line says beauty – quietly. And each line is functional. The low-slung body was designed in wind tunnels for the least air resistance.'

The Karmann Ghia made much of its painstaking finish. Body panels were hand-shaped, and seams between the panels filled with pewter and smoothed by hand.

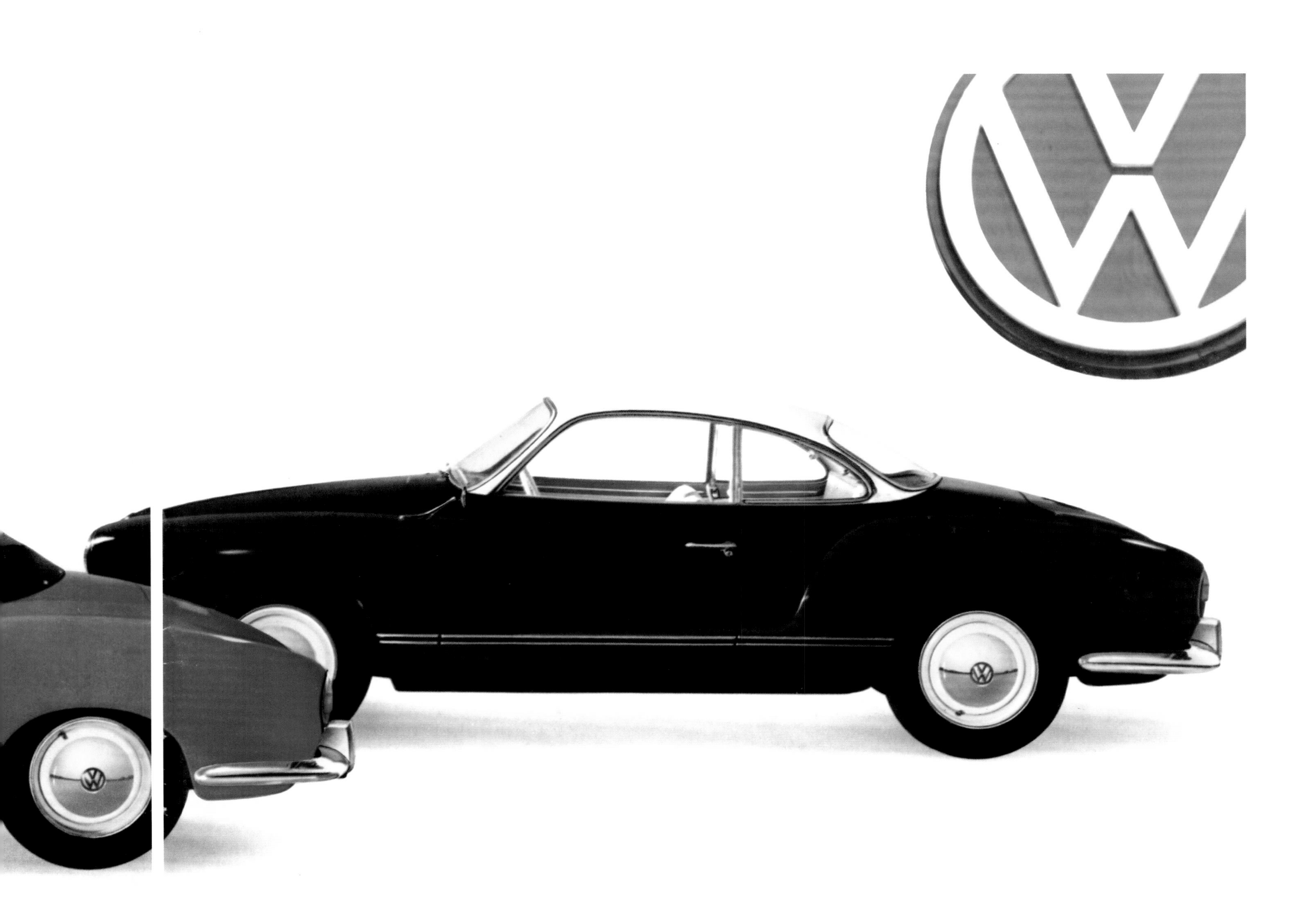

ABOVE The simple fascia of the Karmann Ghia. Maximum cruising speed was about 75 mph.

RIGHT The chassis comprised a rigid sealed unit that gave protection to the mechanicals from dust and water.

Yes, deep down inside it's a Volkswagen. With all the famous Volkswagen features:

The rugged VW engine

Cast in aluminium and magnesium alloys (to keep dead weight down to a minimum).
Installed in the rear of the car. For better traction and direct power to the transmission.
Air cooled. No radiator problems in winter or summer.
Unusually short piston travel. For low friction and less wear.
So precisely built, you can drive at top speed from the very first mile on. You average 38 miles per gallon. Give or take a couple.

The sturdy VW chassis

Joined with the body it forms a single, twist proof and fully sealed unit. All vital parts are covered by a steel tunnel. Protected from dust and mud, water and stones. (As the dotted line shows, the Karmann Ghia chassis is a bit wider than the VW Sedan's.)
Before spraying, the whole chassis is dipped into tanks of paint. No bare metal is left exposed.
You can park your Karmann Ghia in any weather, anywhere.

The flexible VW torsion bar suspension

Four steel tubes (two front and two rear) protect the torsion bars, which flex to any shock and rebound instantly – ready to absorb another bump. Moreover, double acting shock absorbers prevent even severe springing actions from being transmitted to the body. Another important factor: each wheel is independently suspended. A shock to one wheel can not be transmitted to another. Even on the worst of country roads, it is still possible to drive in comfort, with that fine Volkswagen feeling of security you have behind the steering wheel.

The squat, flat engine of the 1500 Karmann Ghia was designed to fit compactly in the back of the car and still leave room for luggage.

**Back up a little.
To get
the whole picture.**

Three things make a car a Karmann Ghia:

- Design by Ghia of Turin.
- Body by the Karmann coachmakers of Osnabruck.
- Engine and gear box and chassis by Volkswagen of Wolfsburg.

The VW Karmann Ghia 1500
is the second Karmann Ghia.
(It doesn't take the place
of the one before; we still make
the original Karmann Ghia.)
It gives you more room than the first.
More comfort.
More power.
Because it's a limited-production car,
it's built like a custom car.
And it looks it.
Example: Fenders are hand-welded
in continuous seams, not spot-welded.
They're hand-sanded, your hand
can't find these seams; steel flows
into steel without a trace.

VAUXHALL
VICTOR

1957 Vauxhall Victor F Series

THE MOST AMERICAN OF BRITISH CARS IN ITS DAY – albeit a scaled-down version – the Victor F was the outcome of combining Vauxhall mechanics with mid-1950s Chevrolet styling, the latter care of General Motors, Vauxhall's American parent. The Victor F was a good-looker.

Launched in 1957 to replace the E-Series Wyvern, the Victor F Series introduced a wrap-around 'panoramic' windscreen (the first English car to be so equipped), hooded lights and those heavy, bossed bumpers. The influence of American styling can also be seen in the rearward-sloping windscreen pillars. The cars were popular in New Zealand, being tough and long-lasting, and were assembled at the General Motors plant in Petone.

The gear change was on the steering column, and the three-speed gearbox sported synchromesh on all forward gears: 'Changing gear presents no problems: a noisy change is impossible with Vauxhall-controlled synchromesh on all three forward speeds ... with dig-in-the-back acceleration when you want it.' The engine size was 1500 cc, and a Super model tested with a top speed of 74 mph. In 1958, Newtondrive semi-automatic transmission became available as an option.

Faced with a growing volume of compact European imports and the success of the local Rambler compact in that market, General Motors had recognised the need for a similar car in its own line-up, and the British Victor was seen as a likely contender. It promised better fuel economy than GM's gas-guzzlers and, with its more American styling, could have an advantage over the European imports. Like coals to Newcastle, huge numbers of the Victor F were exported to North America.

General Motors got it half right. Sales in North America as a whole were rewarding, but more so in Canada (where the Victor F was sold as the Envoy) thanks to the lower-tariff import arrangement that existed at the time between Commonwealth countries, which resulted in more competitive pricing there. In the United States, however, the Victor's uptake proved more difficult, in part because of the small differential between the price of the British model and that of a base version of a larger-sized US car – and the Americans did love their big engines.

ABOVE Final assembly of Victor FBs on the production line in Britain. They were great runners, but like most Vauxhalls it seemed, rust-prone.

VICTOR

'Notice the low glass line and big, panoramic rear window ... And there is performance to match this modern appearance ... the engine's exceptional efficiency makes the Victor a flexible, top-gear car combining vivacity with outstanding fuel economy.'

There was a revamp of the Victor in 1959 with the release of a Series II, which saw a gentle facelift smooth down some of the American styling edges. Then in 1961, the Victor F gave way to the Victor FB – a little wider and a little longer, with cleaner contours and altogether more acceptable British styling. This handsome mid-sized family car drove well and proved very successful for Vauxhall.

With the FB, there was, for the first time, a new sport derivative – the VX4/90. Distinguished by an exterior that featured a coloured strip along its side, a different grille design and larger tail-light arrangement, the VX4/90 had twin carburettors on its larger 1595 cc engine and claimed a top speed of 90 mph.

Replacing the FB in 1964, the FC – also known as the Victor 101 – sported a completely revised body styling that tended to separate potential buyers, some seeing it as a retrograde step after the very popular FB. The FD model followed in 1967, itself succeeded by the Ventor (1968) and then the last of Victors, the FE, in 1972 (which ended production four years later). They were all good cars in their way, but somehow not capable of repeating the success of the first two Victor models.

No wonder this low-swept Victor draws admiring glances! There is grace in every line and value in every one of its many modern features. With a full-panoramic windscreen it sets the styling trend for years ahead. Though built so low to the road—the roofline is only fifty-eight inches high—it still has ample ground clearance and very generous headroom. These long low lines have purpose beyond sheer beauty. Here is road-hugging safety with clean aerodynamic styling which cheats headwinds and crosswinds—making driving easier, quieter, safer.

The famous Vauxhall flutes, distinguishing mark of Vauxhall bonnets for half a century, have been happily blended into the modern lines of the Victor. They now appear, gracefully sculpted, along the side panels.

This is the Victor F Super with extra chrome trim. The car's exhaust pipe ran out through a hole in the rear bumper, a nice design idea, except that exhaust residue caused the rear bumper to rust out.

Design for easy driving

Settle yourself at the wheel of this Victor 'Super' and run your eye over the well-laid-out instrument panel.

Through the steering wheel you see the large and legible instrument cluster. On the wheel itself is the horn ring. On the steering column are the gear lever (left) and the direction indicator lever (right). Mounted lower on the column is the handbrake which has an easy twist-release so that it cannot be jammed in the 'on' position.

Grouped at the right are the master switch, the control knob for the two-speed electric windscreen wipers, and the lights switch. This master switch is unlocked with the door key. The key may be withdrawn and the switch left unlocked. Turning the switch to the left switches on the accessories circuit only (for radio, cigarette lighter and heater fan). Turning the switch to the right switches on ignition *and* accessories circuits. A flick of the switch further right, against a return spring, engages the starter.

The chromium-plated centre piece carries the fresh-air ventilation control knob, the heater control knob and contains an ash tray. The heater itself (mounted directly beneath) is an approved accessory specially designed for the Victor and Victor 'Super' and fitted at extra cost. It heats *fresh* air entering the car through the inlet grille in front of the windscreen. Incorporated in the heater is a booster fan which can be used to speed up entry of warmed air—*or* cool air if required. Extra ventilation, without draughts, may be admitted through the no-draught ventilation panes in the front windows—the lever catches for these rotatable ventilator panes have press-button locks. In the left side of the panel there is a useful glove box.

THE COLOUR RANGE

VICTOR 'Super' Colours

Gipsy Red: Grey and Black upholstery: Pale Cream headlining.

Harvest Yellow: Grey and Black upholstery: Pale Cream headlining.

Horizon Blue: Blue and Light Blue upholstery: Light Blue headlining.

Empress Blue: Blue and Light Blue upholstery: Light Blue headlining.

Charcoal Grey: Blue and Light Blue upholstery: Light Blue headlining.

Laurel Green: Tan and Beige upholstery: Pale Cream headlining.

Shantung Beige: Tan and Beige upholstery: Pale Cream headlining.

Black: Tan and Beige upholstery: Pale Cream headlining.

There are two upholstery styles to choose from in each two-colour combination.

VICTOR Colours

Empress Blue, Charcoal Grey, Shantung Beige, Laurel Green and Black—with choice of two upholstery styles—one executed in Grey and Black, the other in Biscuit and Black. With both styles the headlining is in Pale Cream.

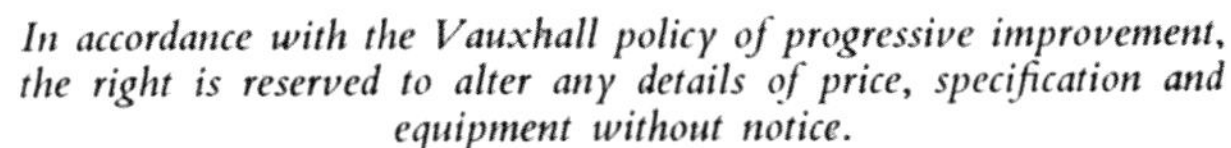

In accordance with the Vauxhall policy of progressive improvement, the right is reserved to alter any details of price, specification and equipment without notice.

VAUXHALL MOTORS LTD · LUTON

ENGLAND

(British Manufacturing Division of General Motors Corporation

ABOVE The Victor FB following its facelift, with the new grille – 'strong, light and, of course, rust-free'. A lack of rust was something all Vauxhall owners would have appreciated.

Prestige car for the enthusiast

Though this exciting new addition to the Vauxhall range shares many basic components with the Victor saloons it has a vivid personality all its own. Powered by a high-compression, twin-carburettor version of the Victor engine, it offers vivacious performance. Designed for the faster than average driver, the VX 4/90 has special front and rear suspension 14 inch wheels (with 5·60 tyres) and front disc brakes.

Four-speed *all*-synchromesh gearbox (with short, central gear-shift lever) and 8 inch diameter clutch are standard equipment. A pull-up handbrake lever is mounted between the 'bucket type' front seats.

Luxury with refinement is the keynote to interior décor. Seats have rubber webbing springs, generous foam-filled bolsters and completely new luxury fabric.

The rear seat has a centre armrest. Grained mouldings add touches of distinction to doors and facia. Instruments include, beside a 100 m.p.h. speedometer, a trip recorder and a rev counter. In the Continental manner, there is a headlamp flasher switch in the tip of the turn indicator lever-switch.

The fabulous VX four-ninety
with EXTRA performance
EXTRA comfort
EXTRA luxury

The compression ratio of this big-bore, short-stroke engine is 9·3 to 1. Special features include aluminium cylinder head, auto-thermic pistons, copper-lead centre bearing, aluminized valves and streamlined exhaust manifold. The twin carburettors are mounted on a water-jacketed aluminium intake manifold. Maximum gross b.h.p. is 81 at 5,200 r.p.m.

ABOVE The sporty VX4/90.

1958
Hillman Husky

ABOVE 'Top of the Haast': Hillman Husky conversion seen on the Haast Road, 1960s. Or maybe it's a Commer Express, which was also based on the Hillman Minx saloon.

THE VERY FIRST HILLMAN HUSKY DATES TO 1954 and was based on the contemporary Mk VIII Hillman Minx. It was shorter in the wheelbase than the Minx, had two doors plus a rear-loading door and a fold-down rear seat, and was fitted with the 1265 cc motor that had powered the earlier Mk III Minx. The passenger doors were memorable for their curious handles: simple catches, yet fiddly, and which you couldn't get more than a finger or two around.

In addition to the Husky, Hillman released a panel-van version called the Commer Cob.

When the first-generation Husky was phased out in 1957, it was replaced the following year by a second-generation Series 1 Husky based on the revamped Series Minx saloon and now looking like a cross between a saloon and an estate car. It had a slighter longer body than the old Husky and used the new Minx's 1390 cc overhead-camshaft engine. Top speed was about 70 mph. Series II and III versions followed, both with improved performance features.

The Husky could seat four people in comfort and still have decent space behind the rear seat for carrying a load. A side-hinged rear door allowed access to a large carrying space for luggage or other items. With the rear seat folded down, this space increased considerably, making the Husky a very usable family car: 'Affection for the Husky is formed within a very short mileage ... Intended for hard work, it is sturdily constructed, yet the need for rugged simplicity has in no way over-ridden the comfort requirements of the driver and his passengers.' Not that they were everyone's cup of tea – they weren't the fastest of vehicles.

But Huskies were cheap and cheerful, reliable and easy to maintain. A review from the time, in commenting on its value for money, said of the Husky Series I: 'A stranger to the car is unlikely to guess that it is the cheapest car in the Rootes Group range as the standard of finish is so high.'

The Commer Cob version of the Husky enjoyed a popularity beyond its basic van configuration. As commercial vehicles were less expensive to purchase than saloon cars, it was a common ploy to buy the cheaper commercial version of the desired car

Good looking
Economical
Robust
Amply powered
Versatile
New HILLMAN HUSKY

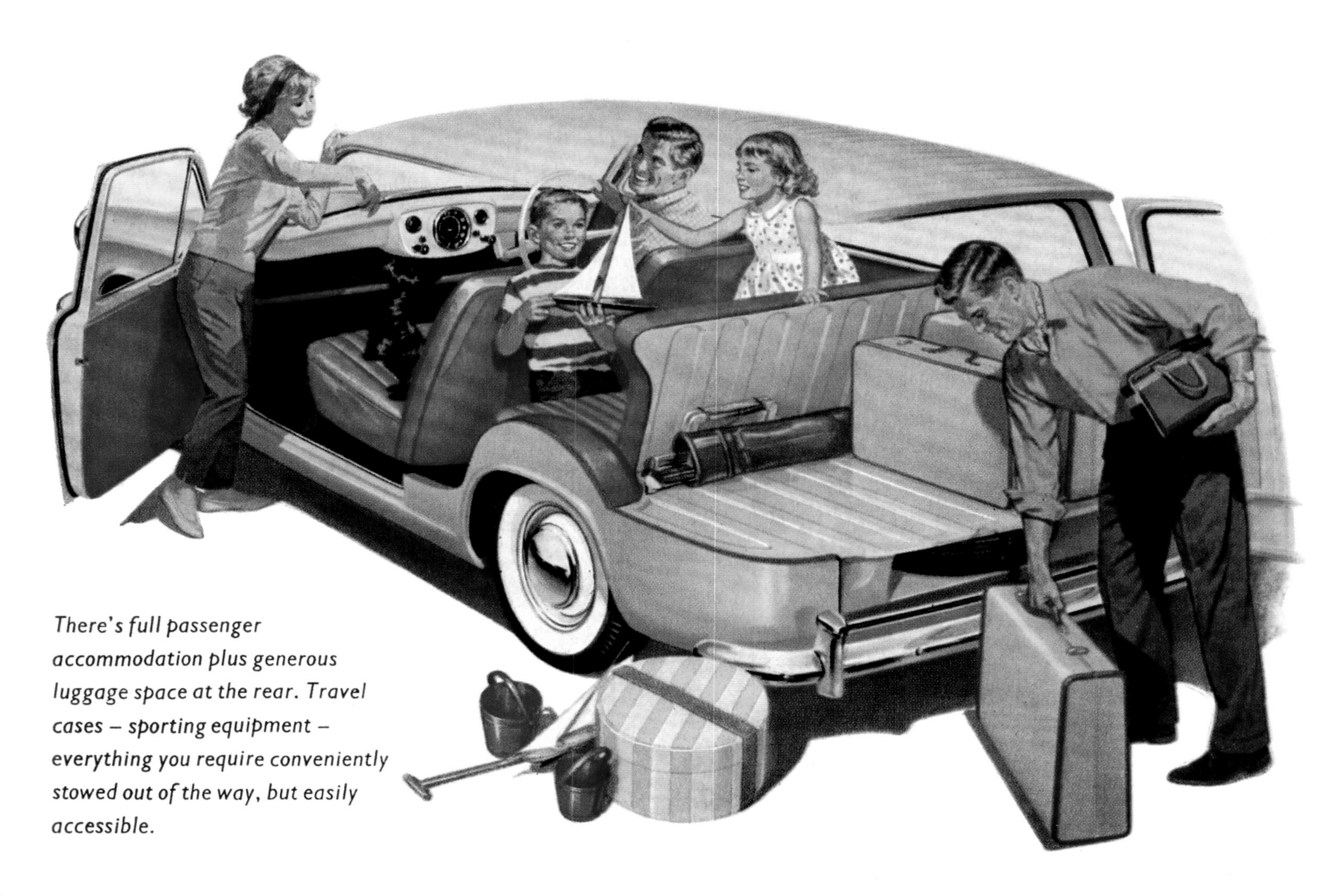

ABOVE A sensibly designed and extremely practical vehicle that, almost without exception, was praised for its strength, usefulness and ease of driving.

OPPOSITE 'A family favourite – a business asset. A smartly styled family saloon or a sturdy dependable load-carrier – such a practical combination is yours with the brilliant New Hillman Husky … in an instant the spacious interior can be converted to handle a bulky 600 lb load – leaving saloon-car amenity for driver and passenger.'

and then turn this into a passenger vehicle. With the Commer Cob, for example, you could get the local panel-beater to cut into the side panels and fit glass for fixed windows, while an upholsterer could add a fold-down back seat. Hey presto, your less costly Commer van was now a Hillman Husky.

Although production of the Minx-based Husky ceased in 1965, that wasn't the end of the Husky line. In 1967, the name was revived for an estate car version of the Hillman Imp, in a squarish design that, with a raised roofline, provided lots of load space. In this form, the Husky name survived for a further three years before disappearing altogether.

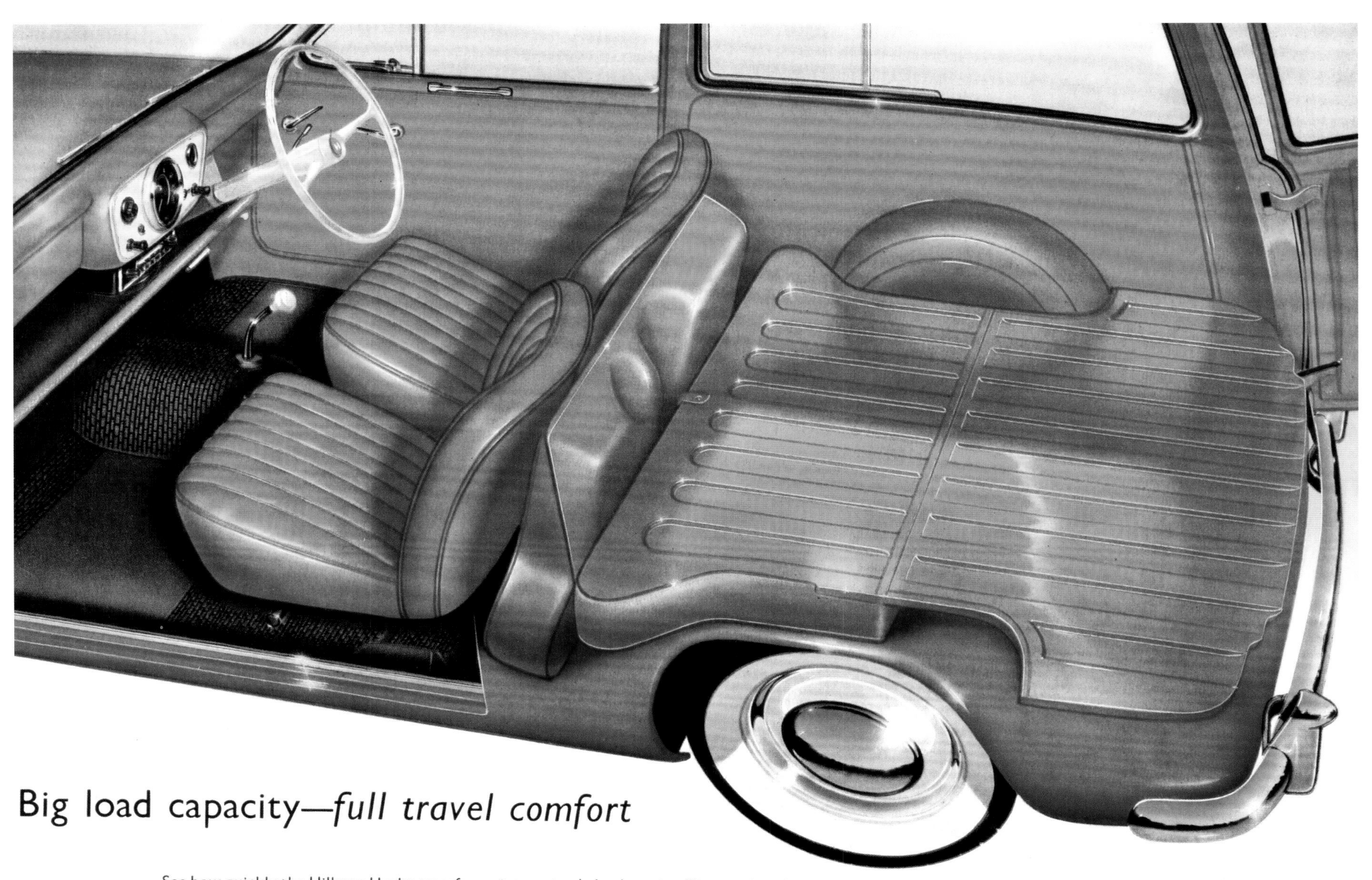

Big load capacity—*full travel comfort*

See how quickly the Hillman Husky transforms into a sturdy load carrier. The rear bench seat folds down in one simple movement, leaving a clear, unobstructed floor space. Now you have a full 40 cu. ft. of loading space, with a strong, solidly built goods platform 50 inches long. The spare wheel is housed in a separate compartment below the goods platform. For the driver and passenger, there's all the comfort and refinement normally reserved for cars of far higher cost. The driver's seat is fully adjustable and designed to ensure a restful, relaxed ride – with ample legroom and headroom.

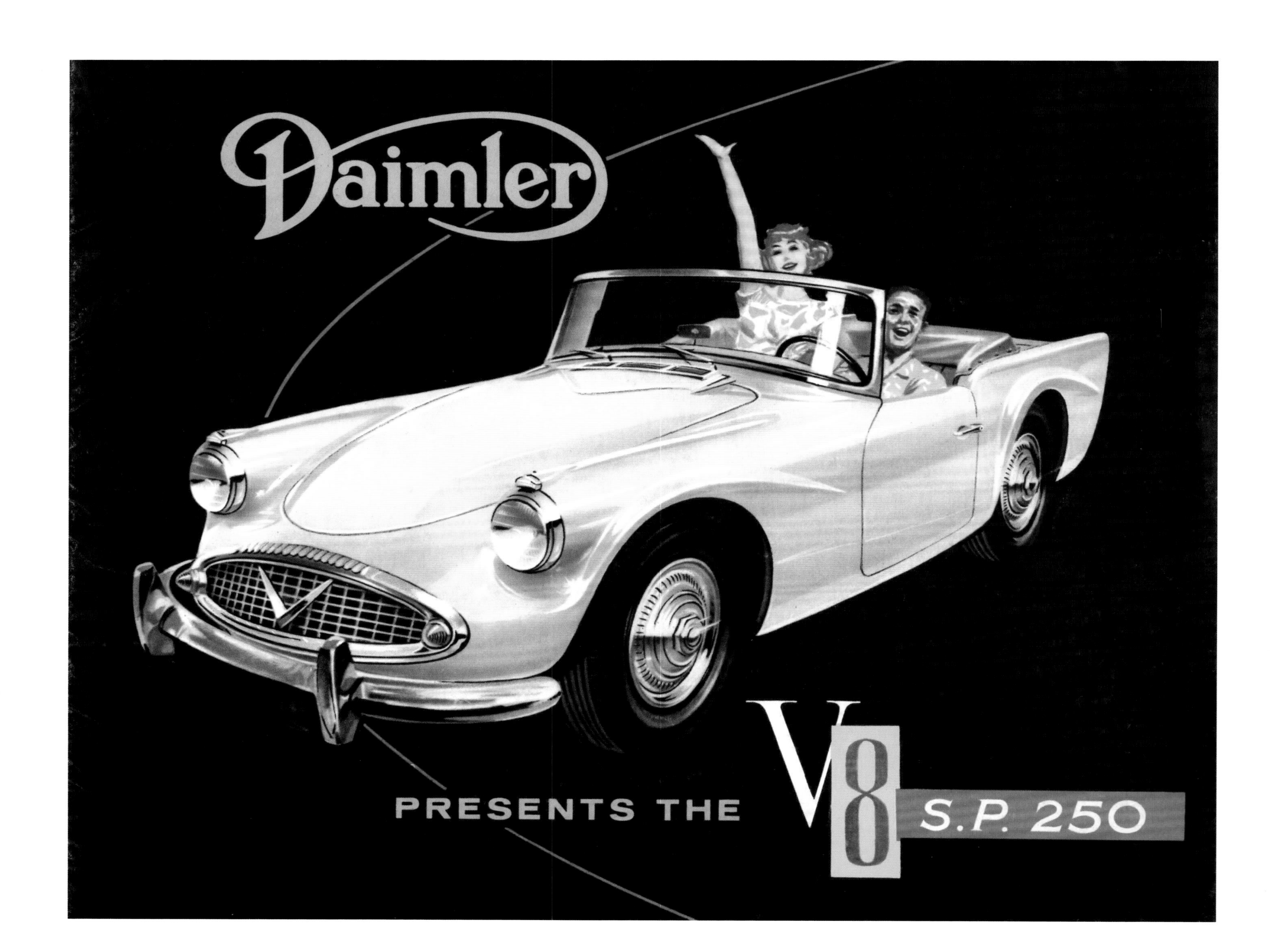
Daimler
PRESENTS THE
V8
S.P. 250

1959
Daimler SP250

When I was growing up there was a Daimler Dart locally. It was black with red upholstery and had wire wheels. There were other open-top sports cars around at the time, but none as classy or as seemingly agile as the Dart. That V8 exhaust note, the shovelling low ground clearance, the diving bonnet line …

The car was always called the Dart back then; I didn't come across its 'proper' designation until many years later. Launched in 1959 as the Daimler Dart, its name had to be changed soon after in the face of threatened legal action from Chrysler, who had trademarked the 'Dart' name. Daimler reverted to the car's project number, SP250, for its car.

The Daimler Company was an independent British car manufacturer that had been founded in 1896 and had bought British rights to build German Daimler cars under licence. The company subsequently became an independent manufacturer of its own luxury cars but retained the Daimler name.

The design and engineering of the SP250 were the work of Edward Turner, already famous for his involvement in other automotive projects such as the Jowett Javelin (page 20). His brief with the SP250 project was to design a car to be powered by a new V8 engine. In addition, the body would be fibreglass in order to shorten the production timeline as well as greatly reduce the costs of tooling. The result was the so-called A-spec., original version of the V8 SP250.

The new car was a looker and it was fast – it could top 120 mph – but its success was somewhat tempered by the fact that the chassis flexed to such a degree that the car's doors occasionally and disconcertingly sprang open. Following Jaguar's purchase of Daimler in 1960, the new owners brought out a B-spec. version, with extra strengthening of the chassis to fix the issue.

The SP250 might have continued in production through many years and evolutionary improvements but for the ogre of model rationalisation, which sometimes followed company mergers. In 1964, the SP250 found itself dropped by the company's new owners in favour of their own E-type.

SP250s were used by the traffic departments in a number of countries – including

Powered by a 'new 2½ litre V8 engine with searing performance'.

ABOVE 1959 Daimler SP250, original specification.

New Zealand, but perhaps most famously in the UK by London's Metropolitan Police. Theirs were all black and in automatic form, and in this pre-siren era featured a bell on the front bumper for use when chasing down speedsters.

Makers of Fine Vehicles for over 60 years

1896 Daimler Wagonette with tiller steering.

The Daimler SP.250 is equipped with a quickly erected fabric top and wind-up side windows as illustrated here. In addition, a stylish hard top is available at additional cost which can be easily fitted without the necessity of removing the fabric top.

Daimler Scout Car—armoured vehicle used by N.A.T.O. forces.

Daimler underfloor engined bus

New Daimler 3·8 litre "Majestic".

BY APPOINTMENT
TO HER MAJESTY THE QUEEN
MOTOR CAR MANUFACTURERS
THE DAIMLER CO. LTD.

S.P. 250

Designed to give the enthusiast owner a truly practical sports car, the Daimler "SP.250" is an entirely new conception which for performance, driving comfort, servicing ease and reliability is unrivalled.

Construction-wise the "SP.250" offers a remarkable specification. Highlights include new 2½ litre V-8 engine with searing performance plus uncanny flexibility—beautiful aerodynamic body in range of striking colors—hydraulically operated disc brakes—carefully balanced suspension giving resilience with pinpoint accurate handling—ample trunk space and low overall weight.

Bumpers were originally an optional extra. Where they weren't fitted at the front, the SP250 had a short bumper strip each side of the front grille, and where the rear bumper wasn't fitted, there were two short, vertical overriders at the rear. Turn signal lights set at the top of the wings above the headlights were a nice touch.

1959
Sunbeam Alpine

ABOVE A Mark I or Mark II Sunbeam Alpine, Worcester Street, Christchurch, 1960.

THE SUNBEAM ALPINE NAME WAS FIRST GIVEN to a Rootes Group car of the early 1950s, and then again in 1959 with the release of the company's new sports car. Built atop the modified floor pan of the Hillman Husky (page 104), the Sunbeam Alpine used Sunbeam Rapier running gear and was originally powered by a 1.5-litre inline 4-cylinder engine. It was aimed at the lucrative market in the US for powerful and characterful sports cars – cars with a bit of romance about them – which that country's manufacturers weren't making: 'Bred from success in international rally events and over the Alpine passes from which it takes its name … with sports performance brilliantly teamed with style and comfort, the New Sunbeam Alpine is expressly designed for high-speed touring.'

The Alpine's look was recognisable in echoing some of the styling found in the mid-1950s Ford Thunderbird, although to my teenage eye the influence was surely the Batmobile used by Bruce Wayne in the 1960s' television series (and the design for which had in turn been based on a Ford concept car, the Lincoln Futura). And the fins on the early models? Not dissimilar to those of the Daimler SP250 (page 108).

A Series II version of the Alpine was released in 1962, the main change being a bigger motor. This now produced 80 bhp and was capable of delivering a top speed of 98 mph. A year on, and Series III cars were available in both open tourer and removable hard-top versions: 'For thrilling, dependable, luxury travel, choose a Sunbeam Alpine Sports Tourer or Gran Turismo Hardtop' – while Series IV (1964) cars saw a new rear styling and the dilution of the fins. The final Series V (1965–68) had a 1.7-litre motor using twin carburettors and pushed out 93 bhp.

But you can never have too much motive power, of course, and, recognising the insatiable desire for new and more from the American market especially, Rootes introduced in 1964 a rocket version of the Alpine in the form of the Sunbeam Tiger, fitted with a 4.3-litre Ford V8. Shoehorning the larger-sized engine into the existing Alpine engine bay necessitated a change to the steering system and, it was said, the application of a sledgehammer in the final stage of the process in order to modify the bulkhead.

SUNBEAM
ROOTES GROUP
NEW SUNBEAM ALPINE

SLEEK · SWIFT · SPECTACULAR

THE NEW SUNBEAM ALPINE

ABOVE Series I Sunbeam Alpine – those fins lent a jauntiness to the car but they were not universally liked. In the Series III, twin fuel tanks were fitted in the rear wings (as Jaguar would do in later years with its XJ6) in order to free up more space in the boot.

This exercise proved more than a little successful, with the new Tiger turning in lively handling and producing twice the power of the Alpine at the expense of only a fraction more weight. And the V8 meant speeds in excess of 120 mph. A Series II Tiger in 1967 had a larger version of the Ford V8. Aimed at the world sports car market, the Alpine did not achieve the popularity and sales its makers would have liked. Competition came in the form of the well-established and iconic MGB, which outsold the Alpine in total by a huge margin – the MGB's eventual sales of half a million cars outstripped those of the Alpine seven times over.

ENGINEERING FEATURES THAT ARE UP-TO-DATE FOR YEARS TO COME

Brilliant New 1½ - litre Power Unit for speeds up to 100 m.p.h. Vivid acceleration, superb performance, with reliability and economy.

Alpine Sports Tourer

ROOTES PRODUCTS

1964 – new styling saw the rear fins much reduced in size.

Alpine Gran Turismo Hardtop

Once again, Sunbeam Alpine keeps the lead. The famous sporting performance is now combined with new advantages and the most advanced sports car styling. Mechanical refinements bring eager acceleration, smooth running and easy control. Greasing points are eliminated. Suspension gives superior road-holding and ride. And Borg-Warner fully-automatic transmission is now available as an extra, alternative to overdrive.
Advanced features include; an "automatic twin" compound carburettor for increased engine efficiency, self-adjusting clutch giving light operation, a fully-adjustable steering wheel, servo-assisted braking with discs at front, and sports-type front seats with multi-adjustment.
The brilliant rally-proved 1·6 litre Sunbeam engine gives speeds up to 100 m.p.h. (160 k.p.h.).
The Sunbeam Alpine is built with fine-precision engineering, to Sunbeam's high standard of quality. For thrilling, dependable, luxury travel, choose a Sunbeam Alpine Sports Tourer or Gran Turismo Hardtop model.

Zestful performanc
sporting successes. You enjo
through the gears, high su
outstanding road-ho
elegance, you have smart ne
is
SUNBEAM

restful travel You have the thrill of driving a competition car, famous for its
performance – swift getaway, nimble gear changes in traffic, smooth acceleration
ising speeds, top speeds up to 100 m.p.h. (160 k.p.h.). For safety, you have
ontrol, and servo-assisted braking on front discs and rear drums. For
l treatment and re-styled rear wings. New hinged petrol filler cap
g. Driving a Sunbeam is a new experience – and pleasure.

Alpine Sports Tourer

This famous Sunbeam can be used as an open tourer or as a stylish, weathertight 'convertible'. The hood can be raised or lowered very quickly – it stows inside the bodywork. The hood assembly is snug-fitting, rigid and simple to operate. Features include: wrapped-round front screen and efficient draught sealing. An additional Hard Top can be supplied at extra cost for this model.

Steering and seats adjustable

The elegant interior of the Alpine Sports Tourer. Adjustable steering and luxury adjustable seats give roomy, 'tailor-made' comfort. The occasional seat at the rear will accommodate children or baggage. Both Alpine models have the sports-type gear lever, servo-assisted foot-brake, organ-type accelerator pedal, conveniently placed handbrake, and diaphragm clutch that needs only light pedal pressure. Rear view mirror has padded frame.

1961
Fiat 1500 Crusader

the medium size car of class

ALTHOUGH NOT VERY COMMON, AT LEAST WHERE I GREW UP, the Fiat 1500 Crusader intrigued whenever you did see one. I grouped it with the Peugeot 404 in the category of 'foreign' (i.e. European) cars, which were all a bit mysterious and clearly from places where they did things differently. What was apparent, however, was the Crusader's sharp good looks and grunty attitude. It wasn't just another mid-sized family car, but one with sporting ambition. And the name was catchy enough, although at the time I didn't realise it wasn't used in other countries.

In Italy, the Fiat 1500 was manufactured along with a 1300 cc model, the two cars nearly identical apart from the engine size, and were known for their power and excellent handling. In New Zealand, the Fiat 1500 was assembled by Motor Holdings and sold by Torino Motors, which also gave the car its unique Crusader name tag for the local market. The Bambina name – used for the Fiat 500 – was another New Zealand label that wasn't used or understood anywhere else. Sales of the Crusader in New Zealand were helped by the fact that, in those days of import controls, you could buy one without needing overseas funds.

The Fiat 1500 was impressive in combining lightweight construction with a strong 75 hp high-revving engine – attributes that would see its frequent inclusion on the grid at motor sport events here throughout the decade. And it was modern in its engineering: the five-speed gearbox and disc brakes on the front were unusual in the early 1960s.

The car's turn of speed was used successfully in the mid-1960s when the Crusader was chosen by the Ministry of Transport as a traffic patrol car. Not many cars could better its acceleration and it could cruise happily at around 100 mph. Traffic police used the Crusader in both Lower Hutt and Christchurch.

Speed and elegance, a panoramic car. Silent

Ample windows all round

Quality engineering

Described as a 'medium-size car of class', the Crusader was stylish (that honeycomb-style grille for one thing), solidly built and fast.

A comfortable interior superior appointments

Separate front seats with curved, adjustable backrests.
Rear seat for up to 3 people. Large map pockets on the doors.

ABOVE As quick a 1500 cc car as you might drive at this time, the uniquely badged Fiat Crusader.

Structure and mechanical parts of the 1300-1500

1961
Jaguar E-type

E-type Jaguar and the Central Hotel on the corner of Victoria Street East and High Street, Auckland, seen in the early 1970s.

When E-types started appearing at the beginning of the 1960s, I took to haunting the local Shorter's Jaguar dealership. Doubtless I tested their patience through my repeated visits as new models in different colours and with different options arrived on the showroom floor, and doubtless, too, lowering the tone the proprietors were endeavouring to maintain. But the E was hard to resist. It was a sensation; visual perfection. I didn't know much about art, but I knew it when I saw it and this was it. Crouching Jaguar, hidden something marvellous. Those lines and proportions ... you just cannot look at the E-type and think of a lot else at the same time. Combining beauty with unparalleled performance in a road car, it is a true icon of 1960s car making.

Jaguar may have promoted the E-type as a sports car, but this was no 'sports car' as we knew it; rather, it was in a separate class altogether. Born of Jaguar's D-type racer, which had racked up numerous racing successes during the 1950s – including three wins at Le Mans – the E-type adapted the D for street use, marrying a dream of a design with the fabled XK 3.8-litre inline 6-cylinder engine. Thus powered, the E-type could lay claim to 150 mph or as near as dammit. And all of this for the kind of money that at the time was just a fraction of the cost of some of its European competitors – and technologically, the E-type was streets ahead of most cars.

The first Series 1 cars through to 1964 were fitted with the 3.8-litre engines, and from then until 1967 and the end of the Series 1 line, with a 4.2-litre motor. It is the 4.2-engine Series 1 that is commonly regarded as the one true E-type, what with its increased performance and the original glass-covered headlights. (Through the 1960s, US regulations on safety and emissions were to have an increasing influence on both the design and performance of British cars sold into this, their largest export market. Jaguar was not immune, and Series 2 cars of 1969 underwent a number of design changes as a result, among them the removal of those glass headlight covers.)

Bodyshell versions for the Series 1 comprised an open-top roadster and fixed-head coupe. An additional model was introduced in 1966, a 2+2 version of the coupe that provided room in the back, leastways for small children.

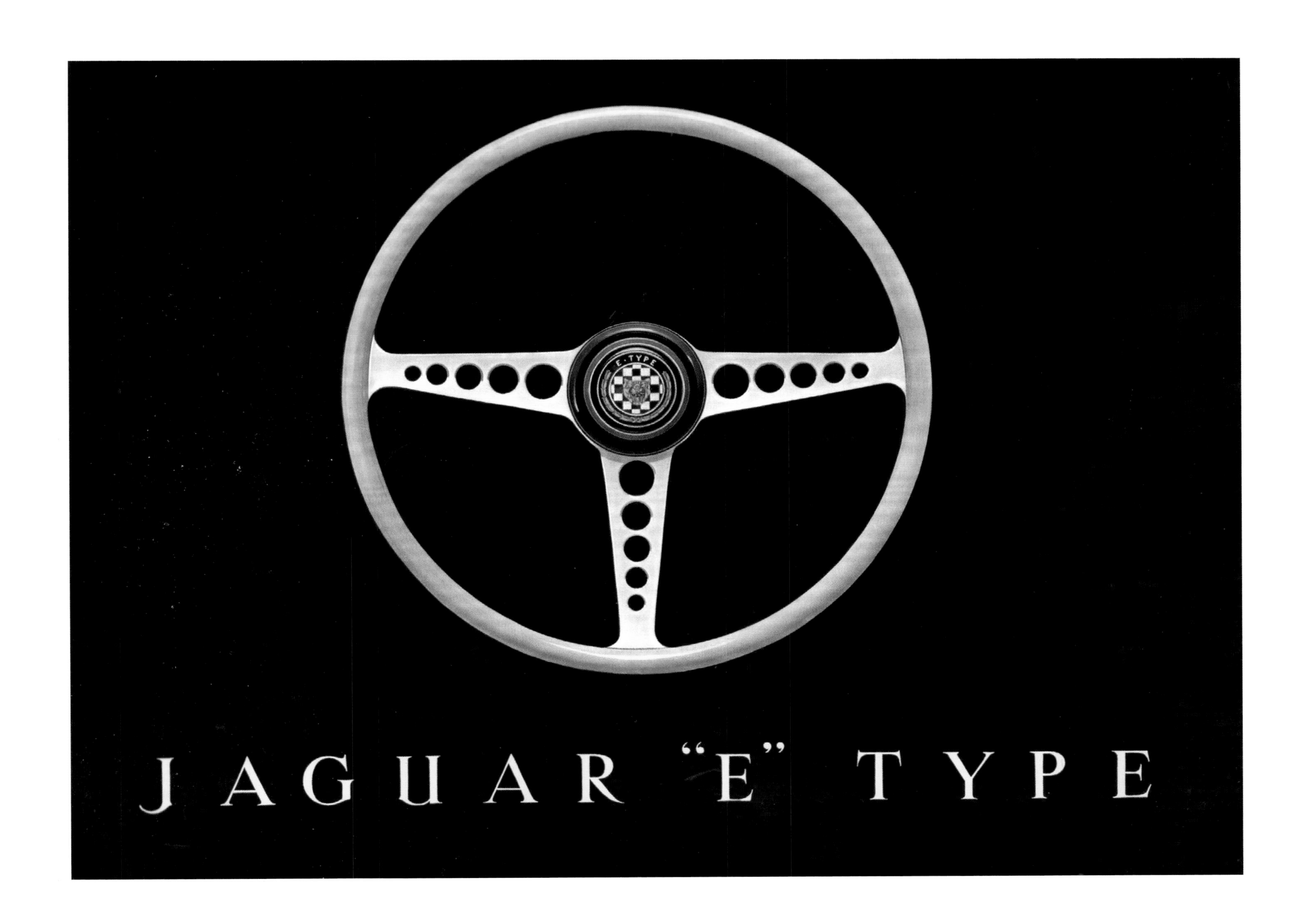
E·TYPE
JAGUAR "E" TYPE

THE JAGUAR "E" TYPE G.T. OPEN TWO-SEATER

ABOVE The E-type roadster in fire-engine red and with wire wheels. While the roadster tends to be most people's favourite, it's a difficult choice between it and the equally outstanding fixed-head coupe.

OPPOSITE The fixed-head coupe – not many cars can pull off a closed-top look that's as seductive as its convertible version. Thanks to its better aerodynamics, the FHC was also the quicker of the two, as if that mattered.

The Series 3 E-type of 1971 constituted a major departure with the fitting of a massive new 12-cylinder V12 engine – along with, appropriately enough, upgraded brakes. The fixed-head coupe body style was dropped at this time, the V12 being available in the roadster and 2+2 coupe versions only: such was the size of the new motor that there wasn't space enough for it in the fixed-head coupe.

The E-type came to the end of its long run in 1974, but it still looks as exciting today as it did when it was first launched.

THE JAGUAR "E" TYPE G.T. FIXED HEAD COUPÉ

THE JAGUAR "E" TYPE G.T. OPEN TWO-SEATER

This sectioned drawing of the open two-seater is reproduced by courtesy of "The Motor" and provides much information concerning design and general construction.

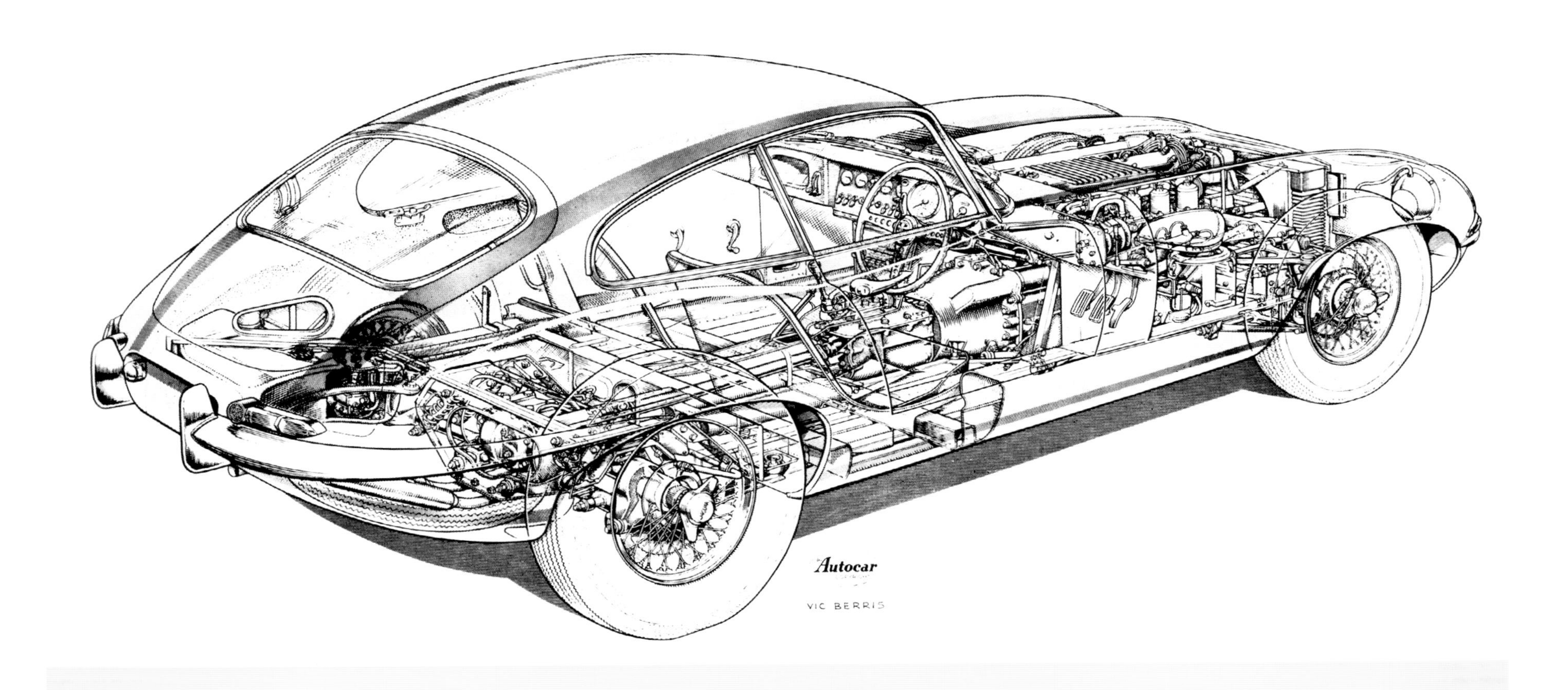

THE JAGUAR "E" TYPE G.T. FIXED HEAD COUPÉ

This sectioned drawing of the Coupé model is reproduced by courtesy of "The Autocar" and provides much information concerning design and general construction.

PUBLICATION No. E. 6134
THE NEW
MG MIDGET
Safety fast!
THE CAR THAT
Starts ahead

1961
MG Midget

THROUGHOUT THE 1940S AND INTO THE 1960S, 'MG' MEANT 'SPORTS CAR', an association that would only be reinforced in 1961 with the introduction of the MG Midget. This little two-seater captured the hearts of thousands. It was cheap and cheerful, nimble as hell, immense fun, and easy to maintain and repair. Its lightweight construction meant that the peppy British Motor Corporation A-Series twin-carburettor 948 cc engine was more than able to give it some decent acceleration and a top speed of 87 mph.

It was as simple a car as could be – side curtains instead of wind-up windows, hollow doors for which there were no outside handles, and instead of a solenoid to activate the starter motor, a cable to pull the starter contacts together. As with other British roadsters, the cabin was a cosy affair with low-cut doors that allowed the driver's arms to overhang the edge of the car, making up for the Midget's economy of width (a reflection of the narrowness of British roads at the time). The kind of car you wore rather than sat in, the Midget was so low to the ground that the enhanced sensation of speed made going 30 mph feel more like 60. It was a go-kart, really.

A larger 1098 cc A-Series motor replaced the original engine in 1962, while in 1964, on the introduction of the Mk II Midget, external door handles and wind-up windows were added. The Mk III car of 1966 ushered in the improved 1275 cc A-Series motor and, finally, a fold-up convertible hood that was now permanently fixed to the car, doing away with the previous tedious process of having to assemble the roof frame, then draping the canvas across the frame, then adjusting turnbuckles, snap closures and clamps – by which time the rain had probably passed.

With the 1975 model, the Midget was given the Triumph Spitfire's bigger 1500 cc motor. The increased output, combined with taller gear ratios, gave a faster acceleration and enabled a top speed of just over 100 mph. In the same year, the bodyshell went back to square rear-wheel arches – good though they looked, the previous rounded rear-wheel arches had caused body strength and stiffening to be lost.

The last Midget was made in 1979.

ABOVE MG Midget III competing in a hill climb at Head Road, Maungatautari, Waikato, 1972.

'You will be exhilarated by the smooth power and performance of the Mk II Midget, a car with a great pedigree ...'

'With sporting appeal from a sporting ancestor'.

Starts ahead

The beauty of the new Midget is immediately apparent, even though the two-dimensional illustrations in this folder cannot do justice to the real car. You have got to *see* it for a true appreciation. For instance, the radiator grille and the windshield and window frames are all polished aluminium, trimmings really luxurious, the doors conveniently wide, and the stop/tail lamps, flashing direction indicators, and reflectors are combined in single units that fit neatly into the extremities of the body on either side. In such detail you find the craftsman's skill.

Starts ahead

WITH EXTRA REFINEMENTS

RPM
MPH
MG

Look into the Mark II  Midget

ABOVE The Mk II Midget, with wind-up windows at last. The square-shaped rear-wheel arches would become rounded in 1972.

OPPOSITE The simple interior, in MG red.

Take another look

at the Mk II specification

★ Space—at a premium in most cars—is available to a considerable degree in the Mark II Midget—there is room behind the seats for luggage, or for carrying a third person for short distances. There is more room still in the boot—plenty of lockable luggage space for your touring kit. Couple it with M.G. performance, instant weather protection . . .

. . . which is assured by the new winding windows and a hood that is simple to erect. The durable and completely waterproof hood blends beautifully with the smooth lines of the car and has a large rear window area for continued good visibility with the car closed.

It's a fast new world with 

– safety fast!

Mk III

Midget

SIMCA
SIMCA 1000

1961
Simca 1000

OVER ITS 17-YEAR PRODUCTION RUN, THE SIMCA 1000 sold more than 1.5 million units, evidence of its popularity not only in its home country of France but also in a number of export markets, including New Zealand. Our family's Simca was a 1000 GL, a nifty little car whose kick-in-the-rear engine, smooth gearbox, and light and responsive steering made it a nimble delight to drive. It was in a primrose yellow, and my father had bought it as a second car for the family when the range came on the market. The price was very affordable for a new car, and for what you got.

The Simca 1000's boxy shape and rearward weight distribution did, however, mean that broadside winds could make things a little interesting if the car was unloaded and only the driver was on board. Having the petrol tank in the rear behind the passenger seat was a factor in that 35:65 weight distribution, but this was easily adjusted by carrying something heavyish in the front boot; the odd bag of sand or cement worked. (Not that there was a lot of room there – it wasn't exactly a usual-sized boot and the spare wheel was already stowed there.)

The French car manufacturer launched the Simca 1000 in 1961 with the baseline 944 cc L and LS models, which had a top speed of around 80 mph. These were followed by the top-of-the-line GL and larger-engine GLS models later in the decade. In 1966, Simca was purchased by Chrysler when the US company decided to expand its operations into Europe (it took over the Rootes Group in the UK at the same time). The new company continued to provide facelifts and improvements to the 1000 model through to its demise in 1978.

There were also modified versions of the 1000, initially from Abarth and later from Simca itself. These took the form of Rallye versions of up to 100 bhp, which enjoyed a great deal of success in motor sport.

The facelifted 1969 model sported new hubcaps, larger headlights and square tail lights.

'From the wheels up, the 1000 has the clean, modern look you expect from French designers. Spick, span and Spartan. Not a flounce to the ounce. Nothing in it or on it that's unnecessary.'

The Simca 1000 was inexpensive and had a fresh, modern look, with a box shape that provided a roomy, open interior.

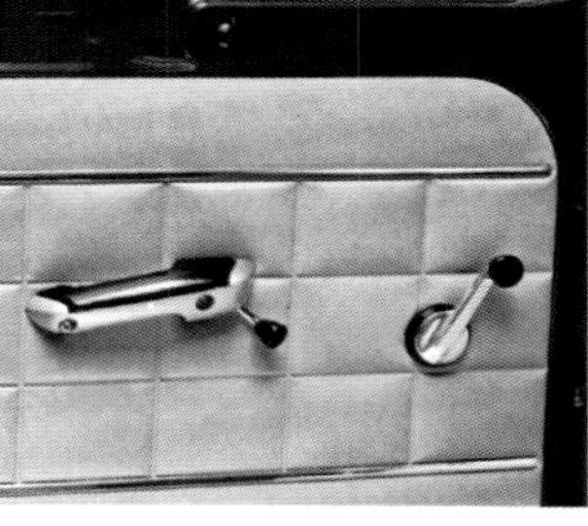

the Simca 1000 GL

A stylish car:

- 4 door saloon with quarter lights on front doors
- functional yet sporty lines.
- five colours with evocative names — Tania green, Nogaro red, Metallic Estoril blue, Eiffel yellow, Tacoma white.

A very lively engine:

- 944 cc, 45 bhp (DIN) at 5,800 rpm. 83 mph.
- 4 speed all synchromesh gearbox (under Porsche licence).
- optional Ferodo semi-automatic transmission for relaxed yet sparkling driving (Available to special order).

A welcoming interior:

- large doors opening at right angles.
- wide and deep seats, designed for long journeys.
- Upholstery toning with body colour.
- elegant and complete instrument panel, finished in simulated wood.
- Optional—fully folding rear seat forming a luggage platform (Available to special order).

1961
Triumph TR4

ABOVE Great fun in the gravel. A TR4A in action in a 1970s hill climb, hard right-lock and pushed to the limit, the driver hoping like hell he's not going to run out of road.

THE TR4 WAS A BEAUTIFUL POCKET-ROCKET OF A CAR, successor to the TR3A. Sitting on a widened chassis of that car, the TR4's very confidently restyled bodyshell saw the old cutaway-door design gone in order to accommodate wind-up windows in place of the former side curtains. In addition, space had now been created for a boot at the rear. While the stylistic changes moved the TR4 away from the minimalist appeal of the earlier TRs, the defined modern lines would help keep it in the front line of sales competition.

The TR4 engine was a continuation of the earlier TR2/3 models (the Standard inline-four engine had been developed from one originally designed for the Ferguson tractor), but increased from 1991 cc to 2138 cc. The standard configuration produced 105 bhp, but in supercharged form and tuned, a 2.2-litre version was good for in excess of 200 bhp.

A novel feature of the new model was the option of a hard top, comprising a fixed rear window with integral rollbar and detachable metal centre panel. With the roof panel detached and the rear window in position, drivers could enjoy open motoring without draughts. This unique roof system would later be popularised by the 1966 Porsche 911/912 Targa, with 'Targa' becoming a generic name for this kind of semi-convertible body style. The TR4 also offered the option of a 'Surrey top', an easily folded and stowed vinyl canopy on a supporting frame that could be clipped into position quickly for emergency weather protection.

In 1965, the TR4 was superseded by the TR4A, pretty much identical in appearance but now with independent rear suspension, which greatly assisted handling. The 4-cylinder engine capacity was enlarged to 2138 cc.

The TR4 ceased production in 1965, ending a run during which some 40,000 TR4s were made.

TRIUMPH
TRIUMPH TR4

Open up!

You've seen the beautiful TR4 body shell, lean and sleek as a sports car should be. Now look in. First surprise : a boot of really sensible dimensions. Capacity? 5½ cubic feet or room for all the luggage a couple on tour would need. And the spare wheel is tucked out of the way in its own compartment. Second surprise : wide doors that make getting in the TR4 as easy as sitting in an armchair. Biggest surprise : when you find this comfort-loving car has all the toughness and verve of a true Triumph Sports Car.

ABOVE Wind-up windows replaced the old flexible side curtains, which had transparent inserts.

OPPOSITE The 'Surrey top' was easily folded and stowed after use.

UNIQUE HARD TOP

The TR4 Hard top model is the last word in sports car versatility—just remove the unique detachable roof panel for open motoring. And for that sudden shower there's a 'Surrey Top' canopy available as an optional extra.

Hard top with roof panel in position—snug and weatherproof.

Roof panel detached; fixed windscreen and rear window remain in position for open motoring without draughts.

The 'Surrey Top' (a folding canopy of p.v.c.) quickly clips into position for emergency weather protection.

Portrait in depth Beneath those smooth lines, the TR4 is a piece of precision engineering with one thought in mind ; swift, safe going in comfort. Backbone of the TR4 is a real chassis of tough, fully rust-proofed British steel. Substantially (right word) the same TR chassis that has stood pounding on the world's most punishing tracks. A little wider on the TR4 for even better road holding and more cockpit room. Next, the powerhouse. 2·2 litres, 4 cylinder, twin Stromberg carbs. This is the world famous TR3A engine, only more of it. Wet liners are fitted, for better cooling at sustained high speeds and lower major overhaul costs. And the gearbox has synchromesh on all four forward gears.

A full range of instruments, carefully arranged to tell you all you want to know at any speed. Illumination is by variable, rheostat controlled panel light. Note too, the ashtray, lockable glovebox and sensibly grouped controls.

What this book can't tell you

The *feel* of the TR4 on the open road has to be experienced to be understood. Performance is certainly there — as good as or better than the earlier Triumphs. And no TR has ever been safer: an adjustable steering column, which yields on severe impact, is a standard fitting. All the facts and figures are on the back cover, and very good reading they make. But only when you take a TR4 out can you discover how this wonderful combination of sports car liveliness and saloon car comfort puts new pleasure into your motoring. Try the TR4 — soon. We don't think there is another sports car in the world to match it at its price.

1961 Wolseley 6/110

'The speed range in top gear is from 10 mph to upwards of 100 mph ... The panel work is smoothly contoured for easy cleaning, and well curved and reinforced for strength.'

'For the business executive or the professional man there is no finer combination than exists in this superb Wolseley, of intrinsic worth and prestige value.'

ALTHOUGH LOVELY TO DRIVE, SOLID AND RESPONSIVE, the Wolseley 6/110 did have softish suspension that caused the car to lean into corners: one writer described driving it as akin to driving the lounge of a well-appointed fall-out shelter – deep, soft seats, and stable as a rock at high speed. It was not for the hoi polloi, however: 'The Wolseley 6/110, in terms of performance and luxury, represents value-for-money unmatched in the three-litre, six-cylinder class. For the business executive or the professional man there is no finer combination than exists in this superb Wolseley, of intrinsic worth and prestige value.' It was a car, then, that reflected British preoccupation with class.

After the collapse of the original Wolseley Motors company in the 1920s, the marque became part of the Morris group and then, in the 1960s – as with so many other British car manufacturers – one of the brands within the British Motor Corporation, itself later to become British Leyland. There, Wolseley lingered on for a handful of years as the top-of-the-range model, before disappearing in one of the many model rationalisations.

The Wolseley 6/99, from which the 6/110 had sprung, was the final of the big Wolseleys. Introduced in 1959, the 6/99 was one of the so-called 'big Farina' cars that had been given the Pininfarina touch when, earlier that decade, BMC had called in the Italian styling house to revamp its range. The big Farinas were updated in 1961, with the 6/99 giving way to the 6/110 and its badged relations, the Austin A110 Westminster and Vanden Plas Princess 3-litre Mk II. Differentiation between these cars lay largely in varying levels of interior trim: in the case of the 6/110, this meant reclining front seats, with those seats having fold-down 'picnic' tables set into the back of them for the benefit of the rear passengers. For the extra money, the Wolseley owners also had the option of duotone colour schemes.

The 6/110 used the same engine as its predecessor but now with more horsepower. The quiet-running 3-litre, 6-cylinder engine had excellent low-speed torque and a top speed at the 100-mph mark. There was also power-assisted

WOLSELEY 6 110 . . . A LUXURIOUS WAY OF MOTORING

ABOVE The 6/110's imposing grille and auxiliary driving lights. The Wolseley badge on the grille lit up when the headlights were turned on.

steering that made light of the car's considerable weight. A Mk II model of the 6/110 introduced in 1964 turned out a top speed of 102 mph.

Production of the 6/110 ended in 1968, by which time the design had begun to look dated in comparison with the likes of the Rover 2000 and Triumph 2000, which had been released years before.

LUXURIOUSLY APPOINTED

The interior of the 6/110 is capacious, lavishly appointed and inviting. Polished veneered woodwork, real leather and thick pile carpets are evincive of Wolseley luxury. In the front compartment the deep resilient seats, of the divided bench type, are independently adjustable for leg room. Each seat is fitted with a folding central armrest. Deep trays below the fascia, door pockets and a glove box with locking lid provide stowage space for personal oddments. The instrument dials are fully visible through the open segment of the two-spoke steering wheel. All controls are conveniently grouped. Positive-action toggle switches control the lights, heater fan and the two-speed windshield wiper motor. The steering wheel is of the dished centre safety type, sponge rubber rails are fitted above and below the fascia and provision is made for the fitting of safety harness.

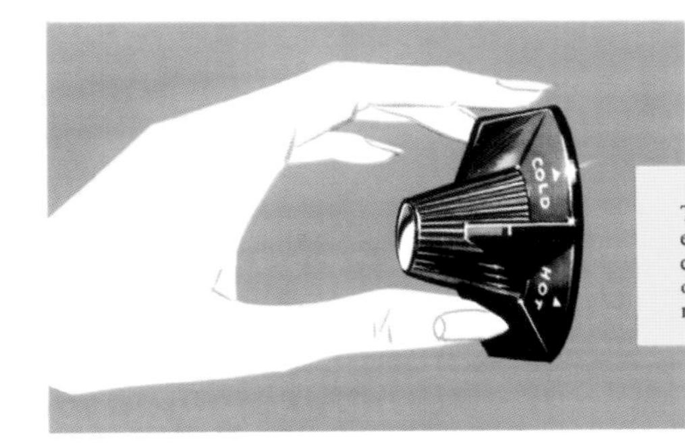

The 6/110 is equipped with a very efficient heater, demister and air circulating installation. Summer or winter there is always a 'just right' control setting.

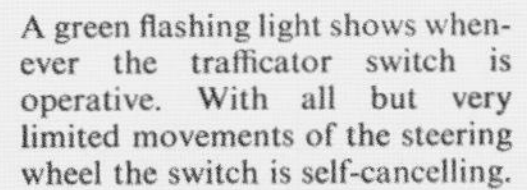

A green flashing light shows whenever the trafficator switch is operative. With all but very limited movements of the steering wheel the switch is self-cancelling.

ABOVE Wolseley cars in general featured luxurious interiors, none more so than the 6/110, which included leather upholstery and walnut-veneer facia and door cappings. In its replacement of the 6/99, the new model saw the gearshift moved from the steering column to the floor.

OPPOSITE The 6/110's body shell with its à la mode fins typical of the Farina-styled cars. A choice of single or duo-tone colour schemes was available.

NEW HUMBER SUPER SNIPE

1962
Humber Super Snipe Series IV

I WAS BLIND TO THE SUPER SNIPE IN MY TEENS, as it appeared boringly conservative at a time when so much exciting new car styling and engineering was happening. But I was missing its under-the-skin class in terms of its build, finish and the sheer comfort of the ride.

Luxuriously appointed and finished, the Super Snipe was at the top of Humber's line-up (the 6-cylinder shared the same body as the manufacturer's less expensive 4-cylinder Humber Hawk, at the bottom of the range): 'For driver and passengers, there is a world of comfort inside the new Humber Super Snipe. The spacious interior is beautifully appointed, with every detail planned to increase the pleasure of high-performance, luxury travel.'

This was an upper-class car, the likes of which bank managers and company directors would buy, slotting in under Jaguars but on par with – or perhaps a little below – Rovers. Solid, British and sort of stately. One acquaintance, after buying an old Super Snipe a couple of decades after its expiry date, found to his delight that the intended targets of his affections were bowled over by the car's quality, spacious interior and comfortable seats, and, not least, the opportunities provided by these attributes.

The Super Snipe line had its beginnings in 1938 following the demise of the original Humber Snipe. It took from that car its bonnet mascot of a snipe bird; the long beak of the ornament had been made of metal, like the rest of it, but this was later replaced with a rubber version to prevent it impaling pedestrians.

Evolution of the Super Snipe first went through progressive 'Mark' versions, followed in 1958 by the release of the new 'Series' Super Snipe. In addition to the 4-door saloon, there were estate and limousine models with a sliding-glass partition between the front and rear seats. The revised Series II model sported a new 3-litre engine, testing at a shade under 95 mph for the top speed, while a further Series III facelift in 1960 saw the Super Snipe given quad headlights and a modern full-width front grille. Styling was further refreshed with the Series IV model, which had a more up-to-the-minute rear window treatment and was differentiated from the Series III

ABOVE Twins promote the new twin-headlight Series III at a motor show in 1962.

'If you have an eye for beauty, a liking for luxury travel ... A delight in high-performance motoring and a regard for safety, the new Humber Super Snipe is surely the car for you.'

ABOVE Luxury amenities included fold-away tables in burr walnut for the rear-seat passengers: 'Two full-length tables fold away flush into the rear of the front seats when not required ... In a centre panel are two ashtrays and a cigar lighter.'

OPPOSITE The handsome Series V station wagon with the new flat roofline.

by its opening quarter-light windows on the rear doors. A final Series V model saw the roofline given a modern flattened look.

Despite Humber's best efforts, however, it was becoming increasingly difficult for the Super Snipe to hold back the years. As with the empire from which it had sprung, there was a feeling of fading glory. A last hurrah for the line took the form of the luxury Humber Imperial, essentially a Super Snipe with a vinyl roof, a nicer interior, and refinements such as automatic transmission and power steering as standard features.

The Super Snipe ended production in 1967, before plans for a V8-powered version had materialised.

A distinguished dual-purpose car - elegant and practical

The New Humber Super Snipe Station Wagon is the aristocrat of dual-purpose cars. Built to the same high standards as the Saloon, and incorporating the advanced new features, the Station Wagon has luxurious appointments, spacious seating for six and a very commodious rear luggage compartment. For heavy or bulky loads, the interior transforms in a moment to a sturdy and efficient carrier which will handle up to 840 lbs. (381 kg.) and still provide full seating for three. The tailgate forms a rigid loading platform enabling articles up to 77 inches (1.956 m.) long to be carried. The large, unobstructed loading space inside has guide runners moulded in the floor covering.

1962
MGB

'Another kind of motoring ... The sleek shape in which you are riding is shrugging the wind like a swimmer cleaving water. You sense the road as something to be controlled and exploited and thrown away, mile by mile behind you.'

INTRODUCED IN 1962 AS THE REPLACEMENT FOR THE SUCCESSFUL MGA, the MGB brought the fun of open-air motoring to the masses and was undoubtedly Britain's most popular sports car. It did for the 1960s what the company's iconic T Series had done for the previous generation of drivers – it made sports car ownership affordable. It had good looks, a lively performance and was just fun to drive, being ground-hugging and nimble, and its proportions and clean lines needed no improvement. The original styling has aged well.

That the MGB got it right was proven by the durability of its appeal across a nearly 20-year lifetime and sales of more than half a million units (including the variants) over that time. It fulfilled the idea of what a sports car should look like, drive like and sound like (think of that roar from its engine at top revs): 'The most extrovert form of motoring there is ... The exhaust lays a deep carpet of sound out there in the open air behind you. A yard away, below the corner of your eye, the road surface is quickening to a blur.'

The MGB Sports was the first model in the range, released in 1962, and was followed three years later by the MBG GT 2+2 coupe. The cars shared the same 1798 cc high-compression engine with twin SU carburettors. The MGB could nudge 100 mph while, because of its better aerodynamics, the GT version was 5 mph faster.

In hindsight the much more powerful 6-cylinder MGC introduced in 1967 (0–60 mph in 10 seconds, a top speed of 120 mph) was one of those solutions for which there really didn't exist a problem. The MGB and GT were already hugely successful and there wasn't a pressing need to make the concept any more attractive. And as it was, fitting the heavier inline-six into the MGB's body shell necessitated revision of the floor pan and engine bay (the revised bonnet design shows a bulge to allow for the relocated radiator, and a smaller teardrop bulge ditto the carburettor), and the additional weight of the bigger engine detrimentally affected handling. After less than two years in production the MGC was cancelled.

A final new model, released in 1973, was the MGB GT V8, which used Rover's 3.5-litre engine. This provided buckets of power, taking the car to a top speed of 125 mph. The last MGB roadster was built in 1980.

MGB SPORTS or GT?
SOF 366H
SOF 368H

The great outdoors . . .

The most extrovert form of motoring there is. You drop onto the sun-warmed surface of a bucket seat, feel it push you firmly in the back as your foot goes down, and suddenly a cool wind is snapping past your ears.
The exhaust lays a deep carpet of sound out there in the open air behind you. A yard away, below the corner of your eye, the road surface is quickening to a blur.

Gravel splutters as you click the gear-change across its gate. Rack-and-pinion steering is light under your fingers as you rail your way through a turn.
Everything is immediate and alive. You smell the countryside through which you are rushing. You taste the sun and dew in the air. You see the sky rolling past overhead.
At rest, you had nowhere to hide from the people around, but now you have the privacy of speed.

. . . perfect driver-to-controls-and-instruments location, with seats adjustable for rake as well as laterally. Anti-burst door locks with flush-fitting interior handles . . .

. . . complete sports car instrumentation, with big tach and roadspeed indicator, fuel, oil, and engine temperature gauges . . .

. . . MGB Sports and MGB GT share 1798 c.c. high compression engine with twin S.U. carburetters . . .

The fixed roof MGB GT 2+2 design provided more space in the back than the roadster – for seating along with greater luggage space. The sloping rear window ran into the rear deck lid, creating a coupe shape and the usefulness of a hatch-back. Wire wheels were an option.

TRIUMPH SPITFIRE 4
STANDARD TRIUMPH
A member of the Leyland Motor Corporation

1962
Triumph Spitfire

THE EVOCATIVELY NAMED SPITFIRE (the end of World War II was still a recent memory at the time, and 'Spitfire' still carried a lot of resonance) was Triumph's response to the arrival on the sports car scene of the Austin–Healey Sprite and MG Midget (page 134). And an inspired response it was, with artful styling by renowned Italian designer Giovanni Michelotti. With its swooping lines, the Mk I Spitfire (aka, at first, the Spitfire 4) was visually seductive as well as being great fun to drive.

Underneath, the Spitfire was at base a Triumph Herald, albeit with modifications to that chassis to cope with the greater demands the sports car configuration put on it. As with the Herald, the Spitfire had a single-piece front end that combined bonnet and front wings, this swinging forward to reveal not just the engine but also the front running gear. The 1.1-litre engine – sporting twin SU carburettors – pushed the lightweight Spitfire at a good clip to a top of 90 mph, the sense of speed heightened by the car's low-slung body. The placement of the gas cap at the centre top of the body aft of the driver, à la motorsport, only added to the sense of the Spitfire as a little racer.

There was a lot to like, the only major niggle being the matter of handling due to the rear suspension swing-axle set-up. If the driver pushed the car too hard, this had the worrying habit of causing the car to 'tuck in', possibly leading to violent oversteer and throwing the back end out. The problem was eventually fixed in the Mk IV model.

While 1965's Mk II Spitfire showed little change, the Mk III in 1967 saw engine size increased to 1296 cc, giving a top speed improvement to 95 mph. A major styling revamp came with the Mk IV in 1970, which gave the Spitfire a cut-off rear end that brought it closer in looks to its sister cars, the Triumph 2000 and Triumph Stag.

At the time of the Mk III's introduction in 1967, a much more powerful version of the Spitfire, the hard-top fastback Triumph GT6, was also released. As its designation suggested, power was by way of a 6-cylinder engine, the same 2-litre unit as used in the Triumph Vitesse. Once again, styling was by the Michelotti studio. With the GT6, the Spitfire finally broke the ton, the new car capable of nudging 106 mph.

The last of the Spitfires was the Spitfire 1500 of 1974.

'Measure the Spitfire by any yardstick you choose. They may come bigger and faster (and a lot dearer). Or they may come smaller and cheaper (and a lot less lively). There's not a sports car in the world like it.'

A newly introduced steel hard top now adds a snug, sleek Coupé to the exciting Spitfire range. It can be fitted or detached in minutes. Just six bolts are employed (two of which locate through the hood stick sockets for soft top use) so that adding or detaching the hard top is an easy, speedy one-man operation.

Complete headlining is provided in Spitfire luxury style, while the large wrap-round rear window gives a panoramic view of the cars you've left behind. The new hard top is available at modest extra cost, as are the chic Whitewall tyres illustrated.

Take all the refinements that usually go only with high-priced sports cars. The winding windows. The luxury of deep upholstery. The confidence of disc brakes. The thrust of instant acceleration. The elegance of Italian-inspired coachwork. The full instrumentation, including rev. counter. The detachable windscreen (for sportsmen).

Put them in a nimble little car with the power to outpace its closest rivals. Add the mechanical brilliance of the famous Triumph Herald — all-round independent suspension, steel girder chassis, hairpin turning circle, steering wheel and facia designed to yield on serious impact.

Assemble the whole with care and attention to detail and quality of work on which the good name of the Leyland Motor Corporation is built.

The result is the Triumph Spitfire 4, a unique new British sports car. Outstanding performance, luxurious comfort and extreme safety—the Spitfire in the true Triumph sporting tradition, has it all.

Measure the Spitfire by any yardstick you choose. They may come bigger and faster (and a lot dearer). Or they may come smaller and cheaper (and a lot less lively). There's not a sports car in the world like it. Marvel at the all-weather versatility of each Spitfire in the range. One of them is tailor-made for you. Spitfire soft top ; Spitfire hard top ; or Spitfire hard top with soft top stowed. And once you've driven one, it'll be the only sports car for you.

ABOVE Options for the Mk I included a removable hard-top.
OPPOSITE A two-seater with style.

ENGINE
TURNING CIRCLE
DISC BRAKES
CHASSIS
SUSPENSION
FOR LUXURY LOVERS

TRIUMPH SPITFIRE MK II

ABOVE The Mk II Spitfire, introduced in 1965.

CONSUL
corsair

1963
Ford Corsair

CORTINA MEETS AMERICAN THUNDERBIRD. The edgy-looking Corsair was Ford's attempt at marketing a performance model at a level above the Cortina, while also trying to extend the company's range when it came to family-sized cars, a niche the Cortina had mined so successfully. The Corsair was to be the Cortina's more adventurous relation and was promoted by Ford as the 'car with flair'. The model wasn't that common in New Zealand, apparently only being imported privately, and examples today are rarely sighted; indeed, there are just a few hundred left in the world.

Launched in 1963 as the Consul Corsair (the 'Consul' prefix would be dropped after a couple of years, as occurred with the Consul Classic, Ford's plan for a whole range gradually puttering out), it was aimed at an upmarket 'executive' clientele. One commentator described it as a 'rich man's Cortina', and the Corsair was essentially a Cortina … with a twist when it came to styling, primarily in that very unusual front end. There was the option of leather upholstery and bucket front seats, and loads of leg room, both front and back.

The Corsair was initially available in 4-door Standard, Deluxe and GT models, with the GT advertised as 'possessing all the outstanding features of the Consul Corsair … the fabulous Corsair GT specially developed for the man who wants the ultimate in performance … a top speed of over 90 mph. Go! Corsair GT; car with flair everywhere, destined to break all records!'

A 2-door saloon and a convertible model were also available and, in 1967, a 2000E model was introduced. This addition to the range provided owners with the 'executive'-level works: radio, walnut-veneer dashboard, thicker carpet and a vinyl-covered roof. It was pitched by Ford as a lower-priced alternative to the luxurious Rover 2000, but of course it wasn't really in that class at all.

Power for the Corsair came at first by way of the Cortina's 1.5-litre inline-four Kent motor. In 1965, this trusty workhorse was replaced by a 1.7-litre V4 engine, later increased to 2 litres. While these new engines brought performance gains to the Corsair (a top speed of 110 mph for the 2-litre V4), they were not popular with Corsair drivers, who found their operation much less smooth than the 4-cylinder

'The new shape of elegance … the car that has flair everywhere. Flair in design! Flair in power! Flair in comfort!'

ABOVE 'Corsair: once a brave adventurer of the high seas in an age as daring as our own. Now, for the man who still enjoys a sense of adventure, who expects individuality from the motor car he owns, who knows what high performance means and will accept nothing less, Ford gives a new meaning to Corsair.'

RIGHT The Corsair's sharp-edged appearance continued at the rear with a jet-like light cluster creating a sort of fin.

OPPOSITE The Corsair looked a lot like the Cortina, but was readily identified by the unusual aerodynamic-looking front-end styling, featuring a horizontal 'V' crease in the sloping bonnet, into which the headlights were set.

Kent. Nor was the Corsair's cause helped when the Mk II Cortina was released in 1966: that car's rapid popularity began to cannibalise Corsair sales.

The Corsair was eventually dropped in 1970, at which time the new, bigger Mk III Cortina took over as Ford's mid-sized car. By this stage, the Ford Escort had moved into the 'small car' spot in the range formerly occupied by the early Cortina. Meanwhile, buyers looking for a more sporting drive – the slot that the Corsair had hoped to fill – would now turn to Ford's new Capri.

434 UOO
CORSAIR SALOON • CORSAIR DE LUXE SALOON • CORSAIR G.T. • CAPRI COUPE • CAPRI COUPE G.T.

1964
Ford Mustang

ABOVE 'First cut is the deepest': the break-the-mould 1964 Mustang convertible.

WHILE A DECENT NUMBER OF MUSTANGS MADE THEIR WAY INTO NEW ZEALAND in the first years of their manufacture, this was apparently mostly by way of private imports. This is exactly what one of my father's business colleagues had done, in the form of a 1965 red convertible with black upholstery. I'd only had my driving licence a short while at the time, but very bravely he allowed me a drive around the block. Those first impressions have stayed with me: the wide, heavy doors that closed with a satisfying clunk, and the car's sheer power (my only basis of comparison at this point my mother's Hillman Imp, which was, in fact, far from sluggish). With just a blip of the accelerator, the Mustang pulled away like a rocket, with that wonderful burbling exhaust.

There's usually a magic with first times that is nearly impossible to recapture – be it an experience or design iteration – and that was so with the early Mustangs; an unrepeatable purity of expression. Of course, the decade they sprang from was a one-off in itself, a time of change, and of (in the West at least) a confluence of rising standards of living, increased aspirations and the spirit of youth. The Mustang was a product of those things and reflected them perfectly, especially in the convertible form: 'Lots of people who thought they could only dream about convertibles now drove Mustangs.'

More than a million Mustangs were sold in the first 18 months of the car's manufacture. While its impact wasn't the phenomenon here that it was in the US, where the price for a base Mustang in 1964–65 was affordable to almost anyone who wanted one, the car still stirred your blood.

Following close on the heels of the first hard-top and convertible models, Ford released a fastback version, with the new 271 bhp V8 engine (most of the early Mustangs were sold with 6-cylinder motors). More power was available with the Shelby GT350 fastback's 289 cu in V8.

A revamp in 1967–68 held a hint of the more aggressive styling that was to come, but there was no lack of admirers of the updated look, including new adherents as well as original believers. Anyone who saw the 1968 movie *Bullitt* is unlikely to forget

MUSTANG!
1966 MUSTANG!
MUSTANG!

'Just mention Mustang and you've set off a lively conversation. All about fun ... excitement ... going places ... doing things. Proof? Over 418,000 on the road in the first year, an all-time record!'

RIGHT The early Mustang was at base a Falcon; it was this utilisation of existing components that allowed the Mustang to be sold so affordably – for around US$2300 – which in turn helped to ensure its success.

OPPOSITE Engine choices for the GT included the 225 hp V8 and 'a real scorcher, the 271 hp, 289 cu in Cobra V8'.

the chase scene down the hills of San Francisco with Steve McQueen driving a 1968 Mustang GT V8 fastback.

A comprehensive restyling for 1969 confirmed Ford's intention to follow the muscle car trend towards models that were bigger all round and had an aggressive stance; it seemed that the joyful, buoyant image of the first designs was giving way to something darker. While the inline-six was still available, you could now opt for a bigger six, and for more and bigger V8s, all the way up to the near-300 hp Boss variant and its Boss 429 big brother, the new Mach 1 model with its 5-litre V8, and a 7-litre Cobra Jet unit option.

In the following years the Mustangs succumbed to middle-aged spread, growing larger and heavier with each model. Eventually, the negative response from buyers led Ford to take the model back to its former sizes and sharper lines.

The early Mustangs were standout cars and it's impossible to look at them even now without a leap of the heart.

10
FORD
MUSTANG
1966

America's Favorite Fun Car

If you thought we couldn't improve on a winner– try Mustang '66!

For '66, we did the nicest thing we could think of—we changed Mustang very carefully. There's smart new ornamentation all around, as you probably noticed on the Mustang Hardtop (cover), Convertible and Fastback 2+2 (opposite). Also new (and standard) are a 5-dial instrument cluster, 14-inch low-profile tires and full wheel covers. But the standard features that give Mustang so much of its potent charm are all here. Plush bucket seats, pleated vinyl trim, sports steering wheel, 3-speed floor shift, frisky 200-cu. in. Six, padded instrument panel and sun visors, full carpeting, heater-defroster*, front and rear seat belts. Plus outside rearview mirror, windshield washers and electric wipers, backup lights, emergency flasher and courtesy lights. And, of course, Ford's Twice-a-Year Maintenance (back cover) . . . all *standard* and all wrapped up in the kind of low price tag Mustang made famous.

And Mustang's long list of options—more than 70 of them—are here for '66 . . . with great new ones like the AM Radio/Stereo-sonic Tape System (detailed on page 5). And nearly all these options are available on all Mustangs. More than ever Mustang is designed to be designed by you!

Just mention Mustang and you've set off a lively conversation. All about fun . . . excitement . . . going places . . . doing things. Proof? Over 418,000 on the road in Mustang's first year, an all-time record! Why? Because Mustang is a personal luxury car, family car, performance car, or anything in between.

So don't be content to just talk about Mustang. From the following pages pick your model, pick your options, then head for your Ford Dealer!

Now more than ever designed to be designed by you

Mustang Fastback 2+2

Pizzazz and Mustang practicality plus! Under the racy lines of the Fastback 2+2 you'll find features that can't be duplicated at anywhere near the price.

For example, the rear seat in the 2+2 folds down to *triple* luggage space. And Silent-Flo Ventilation, standard in the Fastback, provides a continuous stream of fresh air inside to whisk out stale air and tobacco smoke. And with windows up tight, outside noises *stay outside*.

Like all Mustangs, quality runs deep in the 2+2. Seven main bearings on the crankshaft of the 200-cu. in. Six mean greater smoothness and longer engine life. Brakes are self-adjusting. Muffler is aluminized. Ford's Twice-a-Year Maintenance and other service savings, like alternator and Sta-Ful battery (back cover), keep Mustangs out where the driving fun is

To tailor any one of these highly versatil Mustangs to your taste, consider these options exciting new AM Radio/Stereo-sonic Tap System. Ford Air Conditioner. Styled stee wheels. Rally Pac. Deluxe seat belts. Specia Handling Package. And these are just a few

Test-drive the Fastback 2+2. Get a taste o how much a Mustang can do for you.

Mustang Options

Still *more* suggestions to help you "design" *your* Mustang! Mustang 2+2 (above) displays these options: Styled Steel Wheels (with V-8's) and Accent Stripe (rocker moldings standard on all '66 Mustangs). Other options include: Choice of Three V-8's (up to 271 hp!) ▪ T-bar Cruise-O-Matic ▪ AM Radio/ Stereo-sonic Tape System ▪ Ford Air Conditioner ▪ Deluxe Seat Belts with Reminder Light ▪ plus options shown here, on preceding and following pages.

High-style interior in the Mustang Fastback 2+2

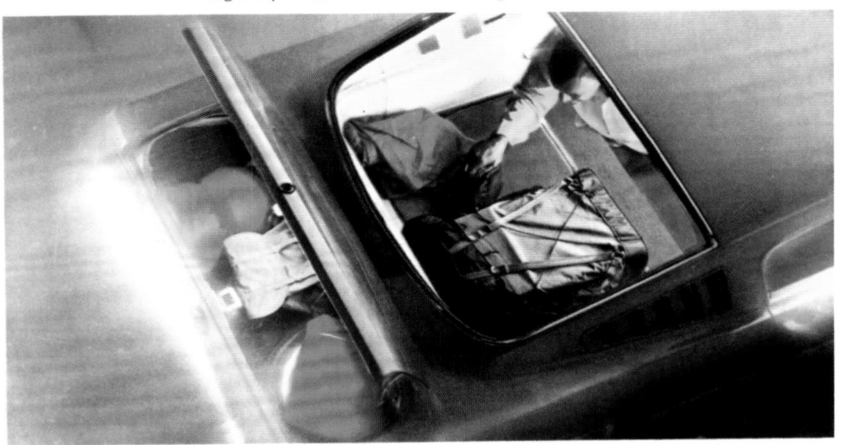

Folding rear seat *triples* the Fastback's luggage space. Door opens to trunk area

1966 Chevrolet Camaro

ABOVE Battling big guns: a Camaro Z28 heads Red Dawson's Mustang at Bay Park, Tauranga, 1968.

MY INTRODUCTION TO THIS WONDERFUL, SENSUOUSLY DESIGNED AMERICAN was at the Pukekohe racetrack in Auckland sometime in the late 1960s. A friend and I, both with ambitions when it came to photography (we had probably come fresh from watching Michelangelo Antonioni's movie *Blow-up*), had taken along our Pentax Spotmatics in the hope of capturing something moody. Life was simpler then and anyone could walk into the pit area to mingle with the cars and their drivers, and we got some great pictures, including a few of a light yellow first-generation Camaro.

I was impressed then and still am today with the dangerous curves of that car. Like the Ford Mustang (page 176) it had been designed to compete with, its lines were, simply, right.

Chevrolet had been blindsided by the huge success of the Mustang, and the Camaro was their way of playing catch-up. The first-generation Camaro was introduced in 1966, available as a 2-door hard-top or convertible. The base engine was a 230 cu in straight-six, or you could go with more power, care of a 250 cu in motor – and then there were the V8 options.

The second-generation model of 1970 was a complete break from its predecessor – larger, wider and with a bulbous hood. It brought a swathe of new admirers looking for a more all-round GT tourer than the earlier muscle car. For many more people, however, the early-year models remain the high point of Camaro design, with the 1969 car considered the best – the classic Camaro.

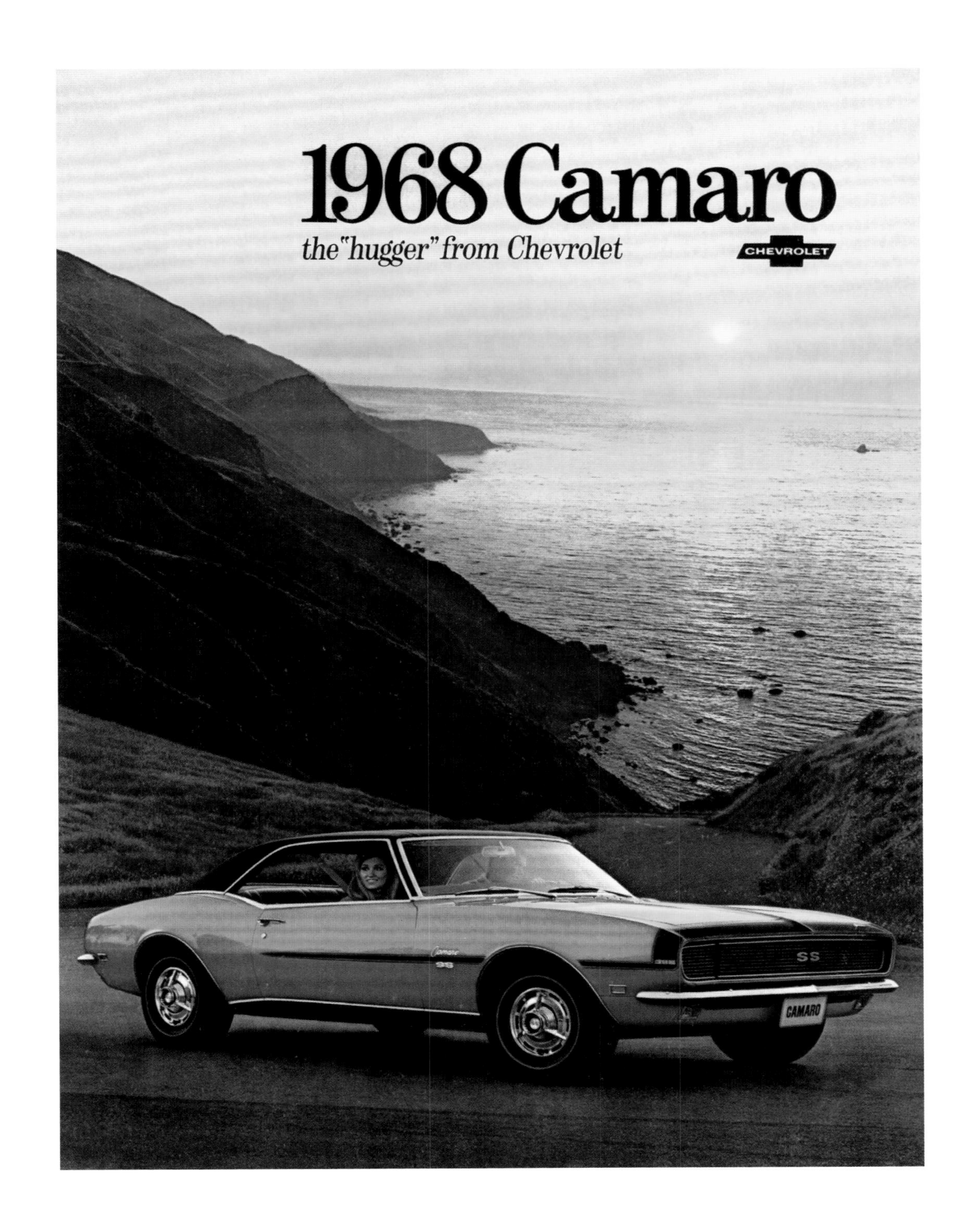
1968 Camaro
the "hugger" from Chevrolet
CHEVROLET
SS
CAMARO

Rally Sport Rally Sport features in brief: • Concealed headlights • Special full-width grille • Parking and direction signal lights mounted below front bumper • "RS" emblem on grille • Back-up lights below bumper • "RS" emblem on gas filler cap • Lower body side molding • "Rally Sport" script on front fender • Roof drip molding on sport coupe • Wheel opening moldings • Belt molding.

Camaro SS Camaro SS features in brief: • Simulated ports on special domed hood • "SS" grille emblem • Special hood insulation and chassis components • 350- or 396-cubic-inch V8 engine • Color-keyed sport striping (black or white depending on exterior color) • "SS" identification on front fender and fuel filler cap • Red (or white) stripe wide-oval tires • Black rear panel with 396-cubic-inch engine • Multi-leaf rear springs. (Rally Sport features may also be specified.)

ABOVE Additional to the standard model were Super Sport and Rally Sport versions.

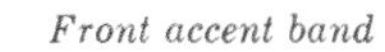

Front accent band

Multi-tone accent band

Rubber-inset bumper guards

Rear spoiler and Mag-Spoke wheel cover

Sport striping and vinyl roof cover shown on Camaro with Rally Sport equipment

FIAT
124
SPORT
COUPÉ

1967
Fiat 124 Sport Coupe

After the sexy surprise that was the Fiat 850 on its release in 1965 – a 2-door fastback coupe in red or burnt orange, with nifty acceleration (but not enough power to get you into real trouble), a wooden steering wheel and a short tail with big circular lights at the back … the whole Italian thing – it was interesting to imagine what Fiat might come up with next in the same vein.

Within just a couple of years the answer arrived in the shape of the marvellous Fiat 124 Sport Coupe, a big brother to the 850, with grown-up power and performance to go with those stylishly sharp lines the Italians do so well. The high-revving twin-cam engine and five-speed gearbox made it exciting to drive, the engine capable of being wound up to the red line before you took it up a gear.

Launched in 1967, the original single-headlights Sport Coupe ran until 1970, when it was superseded by a second-series car with revised styling featuring twin headlights and a softer suspension. In 1974, a final third-series car was introduced, which had new front styling and a squarer rear end, along with a much bigger engine and an impressive 115 mph top speed. As usual, different people had different preferences when it came to which of the three models they preferred, but it seemed to me that the second series with the twin headlights was hard to go past.

And the appeal of the cars wasn't only skin deep. The 124 Sport Coupe was extremely advanced when it came to its engineering, including not only 4-wheel disc brakes with a front/rear weight-sensitive proportioning valve, but also the use of a timing belt for the twin-cam motor, making it the first mass-produced engine to feature this in place of the usual chain-drive. And then there was the five-speed transmission. Engine development, meanwhile, saw the 1438 cc motor of the first-series car grow to 1608 cc in the second series, and then to 1756 cc in the third, which produced 118 hp.

The 124 Sport Coupe ended its run in 1975. As with other Italian cars of the time, it was very susceptible to rust, leading to a low survival rate today.

The clean, crisp body line and performance are in keeping with the dynamic spirit of the true sports car.

ABOVE The Fiat 124 Sport Coupe was an elegant-looking sporting saloon that had performance to match those good looks.

Exceptional visibility all round.

Sports car dashboard.

OPPOSITE Horizontal cluster rear lights identify this as the first of the 124 Sport Coupes.

Instruments, controls and accessories.

Speedometer with total mileage recorder and trip recorder, electronic tachometer, oil pressure gauge, water temperature gauge and fuel level gauge—all with rheostatically-adjustable lighting control. The central console houses the ventilation and heating systems controls and the control for the two-speed fan. There are also variable speed windscreen wipers, an electric cigarette lighter, twin air horns, a steering lock and on left-hand drive models the screen washer is pedal operated with automatic wiper control. Right-hand drive models have a conventional dash controlled screen washer.

1968
Jaguar XJ6

ABOVE Series I XJ6 draws admiring looks at a display at the Dannevirke A&P Show, 1972.

'The least informed man-in-the-street, seeing an XJ6 going by for the first time, would hardly mistake it for anything but a Jaguar.'

THE JAGUAR XJ6 SEDAN WAS A TRULY HANDSOME CAR that made a big splash when it first appeared in 1968. With its sleek styling, effortless performance and roadholding, and superbly comfortable ride, it was an instant classic – the definitive luxury sedan. Power-assisted steering and leather upholstery came as standard, and power was supplied by 2.8-litre and 4.2-litre straight-six cylinder of Jaguar's long-lived, race-bred XK engine (and the XJ6 *was* quick – the manual version had a 0–60 mph time of less than nine seconds). Despite the plush, however, this was definitely a driver's car. Daimler versions of the XJ6 were launched in 1969.

The XJ6 represented excellent value for money and proved popular in New Zealand. Series 1 and Series 2 XJ6s were assembled locally, while Series 3 cars were imported fully built up.

A 5.3-litre V12-powered model using the larger XJ bodyshell was released in 1972 following the engine's debut in the E-type Series 3. This motor provided close to 300 hp and gave what has been described as '150 mph performance and effortless high-speed cruising'.

The first series of the XJ6 ran until 1973, when the second series was introduced. This saw the inclusion of a new heightened front bumper in order to meet US regulations, and a shorter grille, which slimmed the look of the front to create a more modern appearance.

A two-door, vinyl-roofed, pillarless coupe XJ6 was a beautiful addition to the range when it appeared in 1975, although sadly it lasted only a couple of years before being discontinued. A Series 3 model was introduced in 1979 and ran right through until 1992, ending a 24-year production run for the XJ6 of more than 400,000 cars.

Jaguar broke the mould with the XJ6, and for many people it is still the last of the real 'Jaguar' Jaguars.

JAGUAR XJ6
JAGUAR

ABOVE For a big sedan, the XJ's performance was impressive: it was like travelling in a four-door E-type.

OPPOSITE The famed XK engine was available with the XJ6 in 2.8- and 4.2-litre versions. The larger-engine car became the most popular.

JAGUAR

BATTERY
OIL
WATER
FUEL
RPM
HAZARD
REAR
MAP
PANEL
FAN
JAGUAR
HOT

ABOVE An unusual feature were the twin fuel tanks, positioned on each side of the boot.

OPPOSITE The XJ6 was described by many people as the 'best affordable luxury saloon in the world'.

1969
Austin Maxi

ABOVE As well as folding forward in the usual hatchback style, the rear seat also folded backwards. Combined with the fully reclining front seats, this made for very usable sleeping accommodation.

A FURTHER FRONT-WHEEL-DRIVE ITERATION FROM THE BRITISH MOTOR CORPORATION (and also with Hydrolastic suspension), the Austin Maxi was ahead of its time in being one of the first of the highly practical front-wheel-drive hatchback cars that were to become so popular in the 1980s. Its main selling point was the space it offered by way of the hatchback layout, folding seats, transverse engine configuration and low rear-loading lip.

There was much to like about the car. Its 5-speed manual transmission was a notable feature, although in this case what was an innovative system was also notorious for problems with the control linkage – in the early models especially, the cable operation was prone to stretching, which affected control as a consequence. It was a problem bequeathed by the Maxi's Austin 1800 forebear, and which would also raise its head with Leyland Australia's Austin Tasman and Kimberley (page 208), for the same reason.

Replacement of the gear cables with gear-change rods took place in 1970, the year in which the new Maxi 1750 model was introduced. A more highly powered variant – boasting additional 'performance' features such as a sports steering wheel – the Maxi 1750 HL had twin SU carburettors boosting output to 95 bhp and a top speed of 97 mph.

The interior of the Maxi was generous in terms of space, offering comfortable passenger accommodation, but the overall impression was of a somewhat bland car; less-than-exciting exterior colours didn't help. While it was one of the more innovative cars of the period, combining the space-saving advantages of a transverse engine layout with a hatchback rear, the Maxi unfortunately wasn't a success for BMC, and any advantage it might have had as the first of the front-wheel hatchbacks was lost.

The first of the Maxis – the 1500 cc model – were imported to New Zealand fully made, while Mk II models were assembled at the BMC plant in Petone.

Production of the Maxi ceased in 1981.

Maxi
1500 · 1750 & the new HL
BRITISH LEYLAND
Austin
MAXI
MAXI
MAXI

A 5-door hatchback with a transversely mounted engine, 5-speed transmission to the front wheels and independent suspension.

1750

There's one big difference between the 1750 and the 1500—and that's the big 1748 cc engine. Like the 1500's engine, it's specially designed for economy and reliability but with a generous extra helping of power and acceleration.

Both engines are transversely mounted and drive the front wheels, giving the car their compact overall size and uncluttered interior flexibility. Other common features of these two exceptional cars include gas-filled telescopic assisters for effortless lifting of the 'tail-gate' rear door and an automatic reversing light. Both cars are equipped with alternators, protected like the rest of the main electrics by a plastic, clip-on 'anti-damp' shield. Triplex 'Zebra Zone' toughened windscreen and anti-burst doors are fitted for greater safety. A choice of manual or automatic gear-change is now available for 1750 models only, and if you choose automatic (at extra cost) you don't have to give up manual control—this new gearbox gives you both.

There was sufficient space in the back that younger passengers could – in the day when such freedom wasn't frowned upon by the authorities – sit in the boot with the hatch closed and the back seat still in the upright position. Great fun!

'69
Torana
FOR THE FUN OF IT!

1969

Holden Torana

IN THE EARLY 1970S, A COLLEAGUE I WAS WORKING WITH DECIDED ON A TORANA (an LC perhaps, or an LJ) for his new company car. It duly turned up in a pinkish-candy colour scheme, much to the surprise of most of us, who were more used to his conservative approach when it came to colour. But this was a grunty-looking downsized Holden – once you got used to the colour; it certainly went well.

The Torana had its beginnings in the 1960s, when General Motors–Holden in Australia decided to Australianise the UK Vauxhall Viva kits they had been assembling in order to add a mid-sized Holden to their range, to be called the Torana. The first of these, the HB Torana, was introduced in 1967. It looked pretty much like the facelifted HB Vauxhall Viva it was. (Many drivers of the early Toranas wondered at the alignment – or lack of it – between the driver's seat and the steering column, with the steering appearing off-centre – a leftover of the car's Viva origins.) Power came from a 1.2-litre 4-cylinder engine.

An updated LC model in 1969 saw locally produced body panels replacing the imported Vauxhall bodies and signalled an increasingly Australian-designed and produced car. And added to the range was a 4-door sedan. The LC was available with both 4-cylinder and 6-cylinder engines, the more aggressively styled 6-cylinder cars being built on a longer wheelbase to accommodate their larger size.

While there had been sporty Toranas before, things got more interesting with the launch of the GTR model and an even more exciting GTR XU-1 in 1970. The first genuine performance Torana, the GTR XU-1 with its 3-litre 160 bhp six-cylinder engine, had been developed by Holden to keep the company competitive against the big Fords in the Bathurst endurance race. Later models received a larger 202 cu in six with 190 hp.

The introduction of a facelifted LJ model in 1972 brought the Torana closer to the bigger HQ Holdens. In 1974, the LJ was replaced by a new six- and eight-cylinder LH series. Further new models followed until 1979 when the Torana was discontinued.

'The '69 Torana is spirited and obedient.'

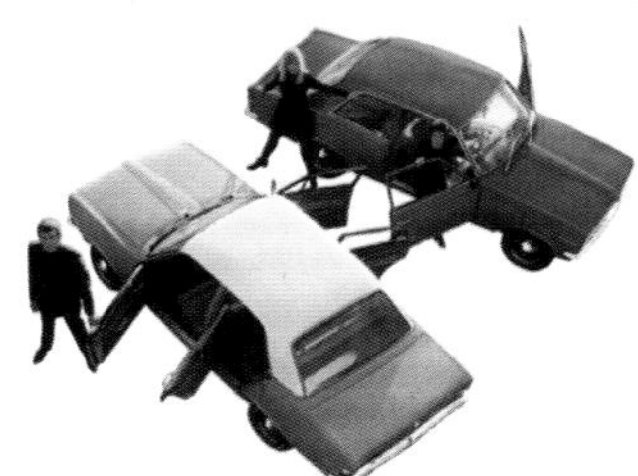

69 Torana has two doors or four.

You choose.

Torana makes itself your kind of car. Two big doors bring out the sport in you; four doors are for practical reasons. Like lifting smallfry in and out. And letting the dog out without having a tail wagged in your face.

In both models, space-curve styling gives you plenty of elbow-room. There are cosy bucket seats for two up front; stretching room for two more in back. And room for a comfortable third.

With the '69 Torana, even the two door is easy to get in back of. The extra sized 43" front door swings wide, and both bucket seats tip right forward. (Safety catches stop them doing it at the wrong time.) You just walk in, lean back, sigh, and relax.

As far as looks go, the pictures tell the story. Two doors or four, Torana still has that sporty, young shape that made it an immediate success. A shape that will still be fresh and wanted years from now when the time comes to trade.

You'll wonder how a low-priced car can look so big. And eager. But that's Torana . . .

'Torana makes itself your kind of car. Two big doors bring out the sport in you; four doors are for practical reasons … cosy bucket seats for two up front'. Bucket front seats were standard for all LCs.

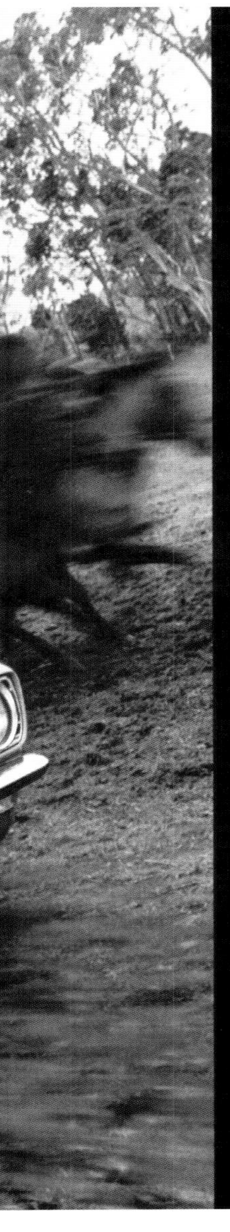

A new instrument panel, with dials deeply recessed to prevent reflections, is standard equipment on all models.

A sporty four-on-the-floor, with synchromesh on every gear, is standard equipment on all models, with console standard on the 'SL'.

'69 Torana is spirited and obedient.

Torana has handling; the thing that makes a car a pleasure to drive. It's quick, responsive, and stable. On smooth city bitumen or gravel corrugations, the wheels stay stuck on the road. There's no fuss, no angry noises: you always know where you're going.

Full coil suspension is the main secret; plus good engineering.

Three years were spent getting it right. And it *is* right. Ask any motoring writer.

Torana lets you play it your way under the bonnet. The basic engine is an eager power pack that does its job for hours on end without complaint. With 56 hp, performance is lively; but petrol economy is just as commendable.

To raise eyebrows now and then, opt for the 'Series 70' engine, with nearly 25% more power for quick manoeuvring in traffic, and safer passing on the highway. Handy to have in hand.

Like the stopping power of disc brakes. Available on any Torana, they're standard on the Brabham, and with the 'Series 70' engine. They stop you smoothly, safely, fast. And keep on doing it all down the mountain.

You can also make up your own mind about gearshifts. Standard equipment is a manual shift on the floor, with four speeds and synchromesh for each.

Its short, sporty action is one of the things that got Jack Brabham interested in Torana. He'll tell you that it's as good as any you'll find this side of a race track.

But tastes differ. So if you go for the 'Series 70' engine, you can also have an automatic shift to make your changes for you. This three-speed unit is already in use on over five million cars around the world. Now it's been specially adapted to mate perfectly with Torana. And you.

From a standing start, the shifts it makes are so smooth that you'll barely notice them. But lower gears are available any time, for sprints or engine braking.

The control lever grows out of a modern console on the floor, with storage space for cigarettes and other oddments. And the selector indicator lights up at night.

See what Torana does for you?

The
Morris X6 range
of vehicles.
Kimberley & Tasman.

1970
Morris Kimberley & Tasman

I REMEMBER THESE – THE 'X6' CARS – when they first appeared at my local New Zealand Motor Corporation dealership. My immediate response was that, after years of Austins bearing English county names, here at last were models with evocative Antipodean references: if I wasn't sure just where or what Kimberley was, Tasman, anyway, was one name I could identify with. They looked roomy – even more spacious than the Austin 1800 that had spawned them. And then there was that impressive 2.2-litre straight-six engine, which continued the transverse setting – and front-wheel drive – tradition of its Issigonis predecessors, right back to the original Mini. (The front-wheel-drive set-up did have its issues, however – like the 1800 before them, the Tasman and Kimberley used a cable gearshift system that could cause problems when the cables became worn and stretched.)

The Kimberley and Tasman were an attractive modern take on the old 1800 – despite a certain boxiness – while to my mind something in the front-end styling foreshadowed the P76 that followed these cars a few years later. Made by Leyland Australia and marketed there as Austins, the cars were sold in New Zealand under the Morris name. At first the New Zealand Motor Corporation imported them made up, but they were later assembled at its Petone plant.

Aside from their restyling, the Kimberley and Tasman differed from the 1800 in ditching the latter's 4-cylinder engine in favour of a 2.2-litre, overhead-camshaft, inline straight-six engine. In its Mk I form, the higher-specced Kimberley enjoyed more power than its Tasman sister, thanks to twin SU carburettors (the Mk II Kimberley returned to a single carburettor, as used with the Tasman).

Leyland Australia's decision to pair what were essentially facelifted 1800s with bigger motors added to the list of innovative new models that company had developed, among them the Morris 1500 and its Nomad hatchback version, and an 1800 utility. Now Leyland Australia was wanting to compete in the family car sector against the dominance there of Holden, Chrysler and Ford. To do this they needed to offer a more conventional-looking sedan than the 1800.

As it turned out, however, the Kimberley and Tasman weren't any real threat

'Both vehicles are capable of speeds in excess of 100 mph ... the cars accelerate in a fashion that will embarrass many so-called sport cars.'

'Before today, luxury motoring has been a privilege enjoyed by a handful of very wealthy people. At least until we built these two new cars. The Kimberley X6 and the Tasman X6'.

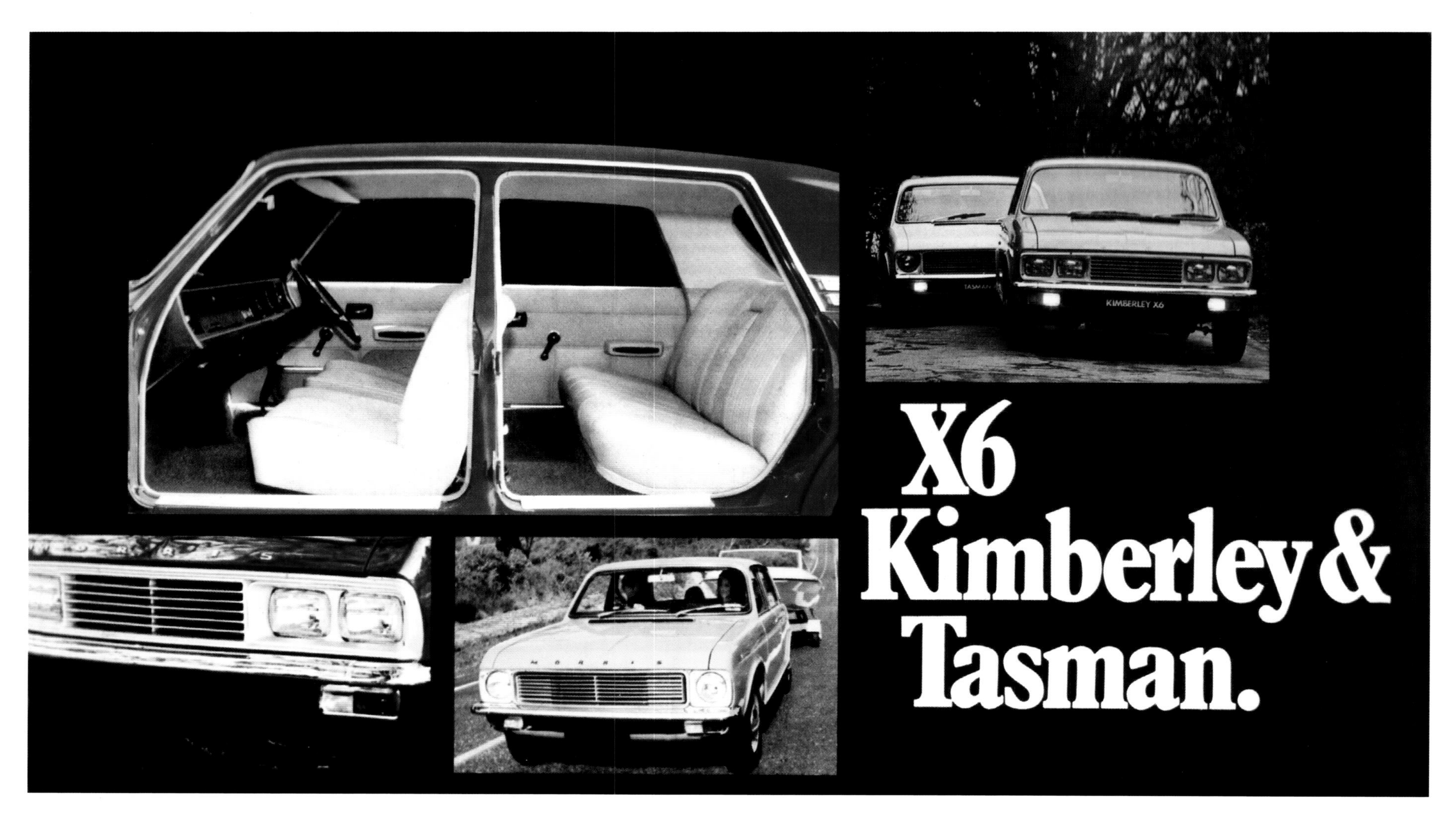

ABOVE The Tasman's interior contained two bench seats that could seat six. The Kimberley had separate front seats (seen here) and sat five.

OPPOSITE In addition to the difference in engine size, the Morris Kimberley and Tasman were also distinguished by their trim. The Kimberley was the upmarket model, with a plush interior and four rectangular headlights, while the plainer Tasman had basic vinyl trim, and a simplified grille with two round headlights. The cars' styling was all new but utilised the doors from the 1800, as well as drawing on that model's design and engineering when it came to the great rigidity of the body. Mk II versions of both the Kimberley and Tasman were introduced in 1971.

to the incumbents when it came to sales. It seemed that Leyland Australia would have to go bigger and make the change to conventional rear-wheel drive if they were to appear credible. Consequently, production of the Tasman and Kimberley ceased in 1972, and they were replaced by the P76, powered by a larger 2600 cc version of the Kimberley/Tasman 6-cylinder motor. The original 2.2-litre straight-six engine, meanwhile, was picked up by the British parent company and used in its 1972 Morris 2200, Austin 2200 and Wolseley Six.

TASMAN X6
KIMBERLEY X6
AUTOMATIC

TASMAN X6
KIMBERLEY X6

ABOVE Datsun Bluebird 310.

Afterword

We are fortunate in New Zealand that there still exists a wide range and good number of cars from the 1950s and 1960s, a period that was arguably a golden age here for motoring. Half a century later, these cars are now classics and are treasured in various private and public collections, as well as by individual enthusiasts and dedicated car clubs. Swap meets, rallies and car shows abound throughout the year.

It's remarkable that so many heritage cars from the time have survived. From the early 1970s, following decades where there was a tight supply of new cars, there was a sudden expansion in availability as import tariffs were dismantled and the Japanese automotive industry increased production, launching more efficient and cheaper cars than those of our traditional suppliers. The result was something of an extinction of 1950s and 1960s cars as we traded in or junked our old motors.

Fortunately, we didn't lose them all; you still saw the occasional old Holden or Mini on the road, and more of their kin could be glimpsed abandoned in garages and sheds. Others were left out in the weather in paddocks and under trees, forgotten cars that lived in a kind of limbo in which they had very little value – often to the extent that it was not even worth the bother of their owners disposing of them. Thank goodness.

Later, when sufficient time had passed for people to wake up to what had been lost, and for the appeal of Hillman Huskies, Jowett Javelins and their like to be rekindled, interest in these old vehicles started to grow again, now with the aim of saving and restoring them. Today, more and more of these wonderful classics are being put back on the road, and there exists a steady market in buying and selling them. Scarcity adds to their appeal, of course; in addition, the passage of time has meant that what might once have been dismissed as clunky and unfashionable can now look charming.

This book and its predecessor deal with the most common cars that were around in New Zealand over the two decades of the 50s and 60s, predominantly of British and American manufacture, with a smattering of European marques. Come the 1960s we also started to see the emerging presence of products of the Japanese car industry which would in short measure go on to dominate the car market here as it would do elsewhere in the world.

The first Japanese models on the scene in New Zealand appeared initially in only small numbers as fully built-up cars. By the middle of the 1960s, however, demand – fuelled by the growing reputation of the Japanese cars for quality engineering, reliability, economy and value for money – had led to the beginnings of local assembly. While many of us may have had reservations about buying Japanese (at a time when memories of World War II were still relatively fresh), the lure of the new cars was irresistible.

Early arrivals on the scene were Nissan and Toyota. The Datsun Bluebird 310, produced from between 1960 and 1963, was one of the first Japanese models available, from 1962. (Nissan's exported cars tended to be sold under the 'Datsun' name; this was phased out in later years and all models were sold as 'Nissan'.) In 1963, the new boxier 410 model was introduced, one of the first Japanese cars to be assembled in New Zealand – by Motor Holdings in Auckland – and a popular choice here. The first Toyota model to be assembled in New Zealand was the Corona RT40 – in 1967 by Steel Brothers' Motor Assemblies in Christchurch for Consolidated Motor Assemblies. A solid, well-engineered and reliable car, it was Toyota's most successful model at the time, but within a few years would fall under the shadow of its Corolla sister. Introduced in 1966, the 1100 cc Corolla KE19 began assembly here in 1968, by Campbell Industries. Corollas soon became the country's best-selling models, respected for their engineering quality and their reliability, and famous for their ability to rack up hundreds of thousands of kilometres without missing a beat (something the old British cars could only have dreamed of).

While we can respect and admire the new, for many people there will always be a hankering for the past, for what progress has dispensed with and left in its wake, and for what has been lost. Though we can't go back in time, there remains today the joy of still being able to see cars of the 1950s and 1960s – unique products of a unique time – standing out in the modern fleet that sweeps along our roads.

TOP Toyota Corolla Coupe SL.
ABOVE Toyota Corona Deluxe.

Acknowledgements

Those who like messing about with old cars are a knowledgeable, entertaining and expansive bunch, and I would like to thank the many people and organisations that were part of the making of this book. From car clubs and their memberships, car enthusiasts in general, friends and family, to illustration holdings and car industry archives, I received a great deal of assistance in the form of encouragement, information and anecdote, along with the supply of illustrations and text excerpts and the kind permission to use these. I am very grateful to you all.

My thanks to: Alexander Turnbull Library – National Library of New Zealand, Auckland Libraries, Bill Riley, British Motor Industry Heritage Trust, Christchurch City Libraries, Colin Campbell, Donn White, GM Holden Ltd, Jaguar Heritage Trust Archive, John Lavas, Kevin Hill, Mark Webster, Max Youle, Michele Cook and the Ford Motor Company of Australia – Archives, Ross Cammick, Museum of New Zealand Te Papa Tongarewa, Noel Stokoe. Many others also offered assistance.

Special thanks go to Colin Campbell, as always a mine of information and resource. Once again my appreciation to Robbie Burton and his team at Potton & Burton.

References

Assembly: New Zealand Car Production 1921-1998 by Mark Webster; Facebook page 'NZ car related street scenes 1950s-1980s'; Wikipedia.

Illustration Credits

BROCHURE ARTWORK

To acknowledge the wonderful artwork of the sales brochures of the period is to not only credit the car companies which produced these – Vauxhall, Austin, Ford of Britain, Jowett, Renault, MG, Nash, Daimler, Simca, Volkswagen, Rootes Group, Morris, Fiat, BMC, Jaguar, GM Holden, Rover, Triumph, Chevrolet, American Motors, Chrysler, and Ford of America – but also to applaud the work of the unknown army of talented copywriters, illustrators, photographers and designers responsible for the creation of these publications. Viewed in time's rear-vision mirror, they combine to form a highly evocative survey of not only the cars described in this book, but also of the period itself.

The brochures were sourced from private collections and from industry archives. For their assistance and permission to reproduce material my thanks go to Colin Campbell, Ford Motor Company of Australia Ltd ('Ford' the Ford Oval and sundry other trade marks are registered to the Ford Motor Company, Ford Motor Company of Canada Ltd, Ford Motor Company of Australia Ltd and/or associated companies (together, Ford). The appearance of these trade marks in this publication does not suggest any endorsement or connection with Ford); National Motor Museum (Australia); British Motor Industry Heritage Trust (All publicity material and photographs originally produced for/by the British Leyland Motor Corporation, British Leyland Ltd and Rover Group, including all its subsidiary companies, is the copyright of the British Motor Industry Heritage Trust and is reproduced here with their permission. Permission to use images does not imply the assignment of copyright, and anyone wishing to re-use this material should contact BMIHT for permission to do so.); Jaguar Heritage; Vauxhall Motors; Coventry History Centre; Jowett Car Club; GM Holden. In a few instances I was not able to contact the originators and/or copyright holders of material.

PHOTOGRAPHS

Permission to use the black-and-white photographs that appear is thanks to a number of organisations, archives and private collections as noted following. As well, for assistance in tracing photographs, I'm grateful to Chris Burles, Max Youle, Donn White, Les Downey, Maye Dunn and Reid Perkins. The source and/or the photographer of one or two of the photographs was unfortunately not able to be identified.

p. 6: Auckland Libraries. Somewhere in Auckland: members of a wedding party prepare to depart in an A40 Somerset, 1950s. Sir George Grey Special Collections, Auckland Libraries, 1269-B728-24 (Rykenberg Photography)

p. 7: Auckland Libraries. Sir George Grey Special Collections, Auckland Libraries, 580-1037

p. 8: Denis Cains. Opening day at Cains Motors, Silverstream, Upper Hutt, mid 1960s. 'My uncle and owner of the service station, Cyril Cains, is the one in the jacket at the left in the photograph.'

p. 9: Alan Boyle

p. 11: Peter Chaney (this photograph is from the slide collection of the late Rex Chaney which is held by Peter, Rex's son). 'This is a photo of me at the wheel of our van taken Labour Weekend 1962 in front of my father's shop on the corner of Purchas and Packe streets in St Albans, Christchurch. It was a CC model with a 3-speed gearbox, synchro on 2nd and top. The wooden body framework had to be rebuilt after only nine years as the chassis rails did not extend sufficiently to support the woodwork – this was a modification we made at that time. The van was purchased new by my father in April 1951. It was used as delivery vehicle for the shop as well as the family transport. My parents travelled all over the South Island in the van for their many holidays. On any trip they would take many of their five children. The van crossed all the major passes more than once - the Lewis, Arthur's, Lindis - and the Crown Range. Note that none of these roads were sealed at the time but that never stopped the little van bouncing across the corrugations or ruts. During our ownership the engine was rebored at 120,000 miles about 1964 – very good performance for a small engine in those days. A lot of the light woodwork body framing was replaced in 1960. My father operated the shop from December 1948 until March 1973. The shop was demolished in December 2002. The van was sold late 1968.'

p. 12: Rod Mehrtens. 'Me (I'm the middle child) and my siblings and mother in front of the family Bradford taken in the 1950s. My dad bought the Bradford from Redpath Motors in Gisborne and we had it for many years, took it to Christchurch when we shifted and to Auckland when we moved up there. We had the aluminium cut-outs as he'd had side windows put in the van; we carted these cut-outs with us on each shift as he said they would come in useful one day. It was a grey-green colour when purchased; Dad had it painted a turquoise green when we shifted to Christchurch.'

p. 21: Auckland War Memorial Musuem. Sparrow Industrial Pictures Ltd. (1953). [Vintage Car]. Auckland War Memorial Museum Tāmaki Paenga Hira. PH-NEG-SP-3-81c

p. 28: Marion Thompson. 'The lady in the photograph is my aunt, Marion Trimble. The car she is standing next to (a Graham Paige I think) was my Dad's. They were at the Ellerslie Races, her father owned a horse called Four Square at the time. Incidentally my aunt was the government's first female Hansard reporter and at one time – and maybe still – held the world fast-shorthand-typing record for women. The photo was taken with a Box Brownie camera.'

p. 35: Denis Cains

p. 36: Hocken Collections. Austin Motors (Otago) Ltd, 1950s. Campbell Studios photograph, P2001-070-001 Hocken Collections Uare Taoka o Hākena University of Otago

p. 43: Antarctica New Zealand

p. 50: V. C. Browne

p. 55: Alexander Turnbull Library. Photographer unidentified, 'School children alongside a Volkswagen Kombi school bus on a country road', PAColl-2647-028, Educational Institute Collection

p. 56: Alexander Turnbull Library. 'Volkswagen Kombi van', K. E. Niven and Co.: Commercial negatives. Ref: 1/2-210532-F. Alexander Turnbull Library, Wellington, New Zealand. /records/23030352

p. 61: Sir George Grey Special Collections, Auckland Libraries, Peter Brennan, Avoncourt Hotel, Avondale. Waitakere Library and Information Services. J. T. Diamond Collection, JTD-24A-03985-1

p. 66: Christchurch Libraries. 'The Watts family (Gus, Ruby, Anita, Irene) from Riccarton, heading off to Motunau for the day and getting petrol and oil on route.' 1969: the petrol station was the Ford McDougall Service Station. Watts family collection. CCL-PH08-HWC08-SO105

p. 71: Museum of New Zealand Te Papa Tongarewa. 'Caltex Service Station, Waihi.' Eric Lee-Johnson; 1950s. 0.011289

p. 89: Upper Hutt City Library, Revelle Jackson photograph

p. 97: Vauxhall Motors

p. 104: Photograph courtesy of the *Otago Daily Times*. 'Top of the Haast'. Haast Pass Road, Otago-Westland Boundary, Stan McKay photographer. Otago Daily Times Collection. Hocken Collections, Uare Taoka o Hākena. P1998-028/09-004

p. 114: Graham Pilgrim. 'I took the picture, in Christchurch, and on my old Kodak Box Brownie, which I would have replaced with a Kodak Instamatic in 1963.'

p. 122: Maurice Cumming. 'This photo of me was taken around 1968 at a VW club Canterbury gymkhana, on an unremembered farm near Christchurch. The Fiat was unplaced being unable to compete traction-wise with the VWs. I seem to remember a Mini won the day. The Crusader I remember had a heater that comprised a rather rudimentary system of a box on the firewall beneath the dashboard which had a large flap that could be folded down to allow the hot, really hot, air into the footwell. It was super effective. The 1500 was a grand little car with sporty performance for its time, although never as fast as the magazine articles claimed. Mine would top out at 88-90mph which was around Cortina GT speed.'

p. 128: John Fields. Museum of New Zealand Te Papa Tongarewa. 'E-Type Jaguar and Central Hotel, Auckland.' John Fields; 1972. 0-030405

p. 135 Richard Armstrong. Donn White at the wheel of his 1970 MG Midget III that he raced during the 1970s at a hillclimb at Head Road Maungatautari. (Richard Armstrong): 'As I usually did, I would do my run and then lope off back to the nearest corner where my girlfriend would be taking pics of me and others and take some pics myself and then back to my car for the next run. If I remember correctly this tight lefthander was close to the start line. If I have got the correct road there were only two corners in this sprint and the other was very quick – those were the days.'

p. 146: Unknown photographer. Roger Dowding was the driver in this hill climb event: 'At the end of the run I had to let the right rear tyre down to get all the shingle out. The tyre had dropped pressure a bit anyway and I nearly rolled the tyre off!

p. 159: Culture Coventry

p. 176: Richard Armstrong

p. 184: Richard Armstrong. 'Spinner Black in the Lexington Camaro at Bay Park on the back straight in, I think, a December 1968 Christmas meeting, definitely no later than January 1969 anyhow.'

p. 194: Unknown photographer